LAW, MORALITY, AND RELIGION
IN A SECULAR SOCIETY

Law, Morality, and Religion in a Secular Society

BASIL MITCHELL

Fellow of Keble College, Oxford

London
OXFORD UNIVERSITY PRESS
NEW YORK   TORONTO
1967

Oxford University Press, Ely House, London W.1

GLASGOW NEW YORK TORONTO MELBOURNE WELLINGTON
CAPE TOWN SALISBURY IBADAN NAIROBI LUSAKA ADDIS ABABA
BOMBAY CALCUTTA MADRAS KARACHI LAHORE DACCA
KUALA LUMPUR HONG KONG TOKYO

*Printed in Great Britain
by Richard Clay (The Chaucer Press), Ltd.,
Bungay, Suffolk*

Preface

THIS book is based upon the Edward Cadbury Lectures delivered at the University of Birmingham in the spring of 1966.
It takes its origin in the debate on the 'Enforcement of Morals'
initiated by Lord Devlin in his Maccabaean Lecture in Jurisprudence read at the British Academy on 18 March 1959. The
more I thought about the issues involved in this debate, the
more clearly it appeared to me that the disputants were divided
by more or less fundamental differences of moral standpoint
and that this fact itself had important implications for the
question they were discussing. For it is characteristic of a plural
society that there are such moral disagreements which run, so
to speak, all along the line; they are differences not only about
particular moral questions but also about the nature and scope
of morality. The question then arises whether the law can
always be neutral where such differences are concerned; and,
if not, how in a democratic society the content of the law in
matters of controversy should be determined. Since much of
the traditional morality of our own society has been deeply
influenced by Christianity, and the law with it, the role of
religion cannot be left out of account. Hence it has been necessary, for purposes of illustration, to indicate what I take to be
the Christian view on a number of moral questions, and this
has inevitably involved some dogmatism and over-simplifica-
tion. I do not want to prejudge issues about which Christian
and other opinion is divided; only to question whether such
issues can always be relegated to a 'private sphere'.

My thanks are due to Professor Paul Ramsey and Professor
Malcolm Diamond of Princeton University who read the MS.
and helped me with their comments. I owe a great deal to
conversations with Mr. J. R. Lucas of Merton College, Oxford,
who also read the text, and to my colleague Mr. D. G. T.
Williams of Keble College, Oxford, whose advice on legal

matters was invaluable to a novice in jurisprudence. I should like to acknowledge a special debt to Professor H. L. A. Hart, whose careful criticism saved me from a number of errors of argument and interpretation. No one who knows his work will be tempted to hold him responsible for the views I express.

B. G. M.

Oxford
November 1966

Acknowledgements

Acknowledgement is gratefully made to the following for permission to reproduce passages from the undermentioned works:

Oxford University Press: *The Enforcement of Morals* by Patrick Devlin (O.U.P. 1965);

Oxford University Press and Stanford University Press: *Law, Liberty and Morality* by H. L. A. Hart (Stanford University Press/Oxford University Press, London, 1963), originally the Harry Camp Lectures at Stanford University 1962; © 1963 by the Board of Trustees of the Leland Stanford Junior University;

George Allen & Unwin Ltd.: *Social Science and Social Pathology* by Barbara Wootton, and *Social Principles and the Democratic State* by S. I. Benn and R. S. Peters;

Columbia Law Review, vol. LXIII (1), article by Louis Henkin, pp. 402, 411, etc.;

Heinemann Educational Books Ltd., and Cornell University Press: *On Justice in Society* by Morris Ginsberg;

Hutchinson Publishing Group Ltd., and Harcourt, Brace & World Inc.: *Sexual Morality* by R. F. Atkinson;

Macmillan & Co. Ltd., London, St. Martin's Press Inc., New York, and The Macmillan Company of Canada Ltd.: *Rules, Roles and Relations* and *Function, Purpose and Powers* by Dorothy Emmet;

Yale Law Journal Company and Fred B. Rothman & Company: *Yale Law Journal*, vol. 71 (1), article by Graham Hughes 'Morals and the Criminal Law', pp. 664, 676, etc.

Contents

1

The Debate between
Lord Devlin and Professor Hart

LORD DEVLIN'S Maccabaean Lecture in Jurisprudence delivered at the British Academy on 18 March 1959 and published under the title of *The Enforcement of Morals*[1] initiated a controversy which has maintained the highest standards of public debate upon an important issue. The two protagonists, Lord Devlin himself and Professor H. L. A. Hart, have shown a degree of sustained passion and clarity of argument sufficient to cleanse the term 'academic' from any taint of triviality or irrelevance. It is a splendid encounter.

All the same it is quite impossible, and indeed entirely inappropriate, to rest in an attitude of aesthetic appreciation. For the questions at issue concern all of us and we cannot take the argument seriously unless we are prepared to think them out for ourselves. And so in this book I want first to consider the basic issue of the enforcement of morals and then to explore some related questions about the relation of law to morality and of religion to both.

Lord Devlin in his original lecture takes his start from the Report of the Committee on Homosexual Offences and Prostitution, generally known as the Wolfenden Report. The question raised by that report is this: 'What is the connection between crime and sin and to what extent, if at all, should the Criminal Law of England concern itself with the enforcement of morals and punish sin, or immorality as such?' The Committee seeks to answer this question by: 'our own formulation

---

[1] My references are to Lord Devlin's book *The Enforcement of Morals* (1965), in which the Maccabaean Lecture is printed under the title 'Morals and the Criminal Law'.

of the function of the criminal law so far as it concerns the subjects of this enquiry. In this field its function, as we see it, is to preserve public order and decency, to protect the citizen from what is offensive or injurious, and to provide sufficient safeguards against exploitation and corruption of others, particularly those who are specially vulnerable because they are young, weak in body or mind, inexperienced, or in a state of special physical, official or economic dependence. It is not, in our view, the function of the law to intervene in the private lives of citizens, or to seek to enforce any particular pattern of behaviour, further than is necessary to carry out the purposes we have outlined.'[2]

Lord Devlin notes that the Committee preface their most important recommendation[3] 'that homosexual behaviour between consenting adults should no longer be a criminal offence [by stating the argument][4] which we believe to be decisive, namely, the importance which society and the law ought to give to individual freedom of choice and action in matters of private morality. Unless a deliberate attempt is to be made by society, acting through the agency of the law, to equate the sphere of crime with that of sin, there must remain a realm of private morality which is, in brief and crude terms, not the law's business. To say this is not to condone or encourage private immorality.'

Lord Devlin notices that the emphasis in this passage is on 'private immorality', by which is meant immorality which is not offensive or injurious to the public in the ways defined in the first passage quoted. 'In other words, no act of immorality should be made a criminal offence unless it is accompanied by some other feature such as indecency, corruption or exploitation. This is clearly brought out in relation to prostitution: "It is not the duty of the law to concern itself with immorality as such ... it should confine itself to those activities which offend against public order and decency or expose the ordinary citizen to what is offensive or injurious." '[5]

Lord Devlin observes, what we shall see to be of importance

[2] para. 13.   [3] para. 62.   [4] para. 61.   [5] para. 257.

later, that 'there are many schools of thought among those who may think that morals are not the law's business'. He mentions:

(a) The agnostic or free-thinker who 'does not, of course, disbelieve in morals, nor in sin if it be given the wider of the two meanings assigned to it in the *Oxford English Dictionary*, where it is defined as "transgression against divine law or the principles of morality"'.

(b) The deeply religious person 'who feels that the criminal law is sometimes more of a hindrance than a help in the sphere of morality...'.

(c) 'The man who without any strong feeling cannot see why, where there is freedom of religious belief, there should not logically be freedom in morality as well.'[6]

This third position is one to which Lord Devlin attaches considerable importance. For he assumes that morality is based on religion, not only as a matter of history, but also in logic: 'Morals and religion are inextricably joined—the moral standards generally accepted in Western civilization being those belonging to Christianity. Outside Christendom other standards derive from other religions. None of these moral codes can claim any validity except by virtue of the religion on which it is based.' It is open to someone who believes this to claim that 'if [the State] leaves matters of religion to private judgement, it should logically leave matters of morals also. A State which refuses to enforce Christian beliefs has lost the right to enforce Christian morals.'[7]

If this view is sound, Lord Devlin continues, the State cannot justify any of its provisions by reference to the moral law and must find a function for the criminal law independent of morals.

This is not difficult to do. The smooth functioning of society and the preservation of order require that a number of activities should be regulated. The rules that are made for that purpose and are enforced by the criminal law are often designed simply to

[6] p. 3.   [7] p. 4.

achieve uniformity and convenience.... Since so much of the criminal law is composed of rules of this sort, why bring morals into it at all?... The criminal law in carrying out these objects will undoubtedly overlap the moral law. Crimes of violence are morally wrong and they are also offences against good order; therefore they offend against both laws. But this is simply because the two laws in pursuit of different objectives happen to cover the same area. Such is the argument.[8]

Lord Devlin is not happy with this argument. He feels, to use his own words again, that 'a complete separation of crime from sin ... would not be good for the moral law and might be disastrous for the criminal'.[9] But can this feeling be justified? He sets out to show that it can, and the very attempt to do this, quite apart from the positive thesis which he puts forward, alarms some of his critics. Thus Mr. Graham Hughes commented in the *Yale Law Journal* 1961:[10]

The feature of Lord Devlin's lecture that aroused most interest and generated most heat was that his central thesis appeared to be an attack on a view of the nature and function of the criminal law which had been accepted for so long by an important section of public opinion that it might fairly be called orthodoxy on this point. The position under attack is the utilitarian or Benthamite view of morality and law.

In order to test this conception of the function of the criminal law Lord Devlin proceeds to ask whether it is consistent with the principles and practice of English criminal law as it exists today. This is for him only a starting point for he does not assume (and none of his critics accuses him of assuming) that English law as it exists today is beyond criticism. He claims that it *is* inconsistent with English criminal law on one point of fundamental principle, namely, that the law will not permit consent of the victim to be used as a defence. 'It is not a defence to any form of assault that the victim thought his punishment well deserved and submitted to it; to make a good defence the accused must prove that the law gave him the right to chastise and that he exercised it reasonably.'[11] 'There is', he goes on, 'only one explanation of what has hitherto been accepted as the basis of the criminal law and that is that there are certain standards of behaviour or moral principles which society requires to be observed; and the breach of them is an offence not merely against the person who is injured but against society as a whole.' Among these principles is that of the sanctity of human life.

Thus if the law were to be reformed so as to eliminate from it everything that was not designed to preserve order and decency or to protect citizens (including the protection of youth from corruption) the effect would be to overturn a fundamental principle. It would also result in the abolition of a number of specific crimes—euthanasia, suicide,[12] attempted suicide and suicide pacts, duelling, abortion, incest between brother and sister. These 'are all acts which can be done in private and without offence to others and need not involve the corruption or exploitation of others'.[13] In some of these cases the law may need reform, but no one suggests that they should all be left outside the scope of the law as matters of private morality. 'They can be brought within it only as a matter of moral principle.'[14] Moreover, the fact that the law will not protect those engaged in immorality of any sort (e.g. letting a house for immoral purposes) can only be explained on the basis that the law has a concern with morality as such.

What then is the justification, if any, for this concern? Lord Devlin proposes to consider three questions:

'(1) Has society the right to pass judgement at all on matters of morals? Ought there, in other words, to be a public morality, or are morals always a matter for private judgement?

'(2) If society has the right to pass judgement, has it also the right to use the weapon of the law to enforce it?

'(3) If so, ought it to use that weapon in all cases or only in some; and if only in some, on what principles should it distinguish?'[15]

---

[12] Suicide and attempted suicide have ceased to be crimes since this discussion was initiated.
[13] p. 7.   [14] p. 7.   [15] p. 7.

It is in answering the first and second of these questions that
Lord Devlin develops the thesis which has aroused most controversy. He answers them both in the affirmative. In considering the first he relies upon two arguments. The first of these is,
in effect, an *ad hominem* argument against the Wolfenden
Committee. Unless society is prepared to say that homosexuality is wrong there would be no basis for a law protecting
youth from 'corruption' or punishing a man for living on
'immoral' earnings of a male prostitute. Lord Devlin claims to
discover an ambiguity in the language of the Report. 'Is the
"freedom of choice and action" that is offered to the individual,
freedom to decide for himself what is moral or immoral,
society remaining neutral; or is it freedom to be immoral if he
wants to be?'[16] There is no ambiguity, however, in the committee's conclusion which presupposes that society does hold
homosexuality to be morally wrong. The second is an *a priori*
argument; that what makes a collection of individuals a society
is a shared morality. The most striking illustrations of this are
institutions such as marriage. 'Whether a man should be
allowed to take more than one wife is something about which
every society has to make up its mind one way or the other.'[17]
Marriage is a clear case of the relation between politics and
morals, since it is part of the structure of our society, and also
the basis of a moral code which condemns adultery and fornica-
tion. However, public morality is not confined to what supports
institutions. 'If men and women try to create a society in which
there is no fundamental agreement about good and evil they
will fail; if, having based it on common agreement, the agreement goes, the society will disintegrate.'[18]

The answer to the second question is now clear: '... If
society has a right to make a judgement and has it on the
basis that a recognized morality is as necessary to society as,
say, a recognized government, then society may use the law to
preserve morality *in the same way as it uses it to safeguard
anything else that is essential to its existence*'[19] (my italics).
It follows that it is not possible to set theoretical limits to the

[16] p. 8.   [17] p. 9.   [18] p. 10.   [19] p. 11.

power of the State to legislate against immorality. 'The suppression of vice is as much the law's business as the suppression of subversive activities; it is no more possible to define a sphere of private morality than it is to define one of private subversive activity.'[20] The analogy with treason is one which Lord Devlin emphasizes but we should notice that it is not made to bear the whole weight of his argument against the conception of 'private immoral activity'. He argues that such activity would have to be of a kind that is in its nature incapable of injuring society. Drunkenness might seem to be a case, but, 'suppose a quarter or a half of the population got drunk every night, what sort of society would it be? You cannot set a theoretical limit to the number of people who can get drunk before society is entitled to legislate against drunkenness. The same may be said of gambling.'[21]

Before proceeding to the third and last question as to the principles to be used in determining what sorts of immoral activity should be prohibited by law, Lord Devlin addresses himself to the problem of *ascertaining* the moral judgements of society. It is necessary to note carefully what he says about this, since it has been as fiercely controverted as the principal thesis itself. It is not, he says, to be done by counting heads, but by using a standard which has been evolved by English law, that of the reasonable or right-minded man—'the man on the Clapham omnibus', or the man in the jury box. 'For the moral judgement of society must be something about which any twelve men or women drawn at random might after discussion be expected to be unanimous.'[22] 'Immorality, ... for the purpose of the law, is what every right-minded person is presumed to consider to be immoral.'[23]

Any immorality is capable, in principle, of affecting society injuriously, but a line has in practice to be drawn. The third question concerns the principles upon which this should be done. Morality is a sphere in which there is a public interest but 'the individual has a *locus standi* too; he cannot be expected to surrender to the judgement of society the whole con-

[20] p. 14.   [21] p. 14.   [22] p. 15.   [23] p. 15.

B

duct of his life. It is the old and familiar question of striking a balance between the rights and interests of society and those of the individual.'[24] Nevertheless it is possible to lay down some general principles. Lord Devlin enumerates four of them:

(1) There must be toleration of the maximum individual freedom that is consistent with the integrity of society. This is a principle which applies, not indeed to the whole of the criminal law, but to that part of it which is concerned with matters of conscience. Lord Devlin believes that most people would agree with it. But he places a gloss upon it whose status is not immediately clear:

The principle appears to me to be peculiarly appropriate to all questions of morals. Nothing should be punished by the law that does not lie beyond the limits of tolerance. It is not nearly enough to say that the majority dislike a practice; there must be a real feeling of reprobation. Those who are dissatisfied with the present law on homosexuality often say that the opponents of reform are swayed simply by disgust. If that were so it would be wrong, but I do not think one can ignore disgust if it is deeply felt and not manufactured. Its presence is a good indication that the bounds of toleration are being reached. Not everything is to be tolerated. No society can do without intolerance, indignation, and disgust; they are the forces behind the moral law. . .[25]

'Nothing should be punished by the law that does not lie beyond the limits of tolerance.' The limits of tolerance are, it would seem, those beyond which the integrity of society is threatened, so that this principle is simply a reformulation of the other. What then is the relevance of feelings of reprobation and disgust? It is, presumably, that they are good indications that the limits of toleration are being reached, i.e. that the point has come when the integrity of society is being threatened. Lord Devlin in his preface replies to some criticisms of this passage. 'It must be read in subjection to the statement that the judgement which the community passes on a practice which it dislikes must be calm and dispassionate and that mere disapproval is not enough to justify interference.'[26] 'To assert or to imply—both assertion and implication have been very

[24] p. 15.   [25] p. 17.   [26] p. ix.

frequently employed—that the author would like to see the criminal law used to stamp out whatever makes the ordinary man sick hardly does justice to the argument.'[27]

(2) The limits of tolerance shift. This represents another principle which law makers should bear in mind. 'I suppose that moral standards do not shift; so far as they come from divine revelation they do not, and I am willing to assume that the moral judgements made by society always remain good for that society. But the extent to which society will tolerate—I mean tolerate, not approve—departures from moral standards varies from generation to generation.'[28] It follows, Lord Devlin thinks, that the law should be slow to move, although it should sometimes move in the end.

(3) As far as possible privacy should be respected. This consideration does not justify the exclusion of all private immorality from the scope of the law, but it does mean that the claims of privacy have independent weight as against the public interest.[29]

(4) The law is concerned with a minimum and not with a maximum standard of behaviour. 'No man is worth much who regulates his conduct with the sole object of escaping punishment, and every worthy society sets for its members standards

---

[27] p. viii.   [28] p. 18.

[29] It will be noticed that 'private immorality' here has a different sense from that given it by the Wolfenden Committee. The expression 'private morality' is used in a number of different senses in the course of this debate, and it may be useful at this stage to distinguish three of them.

(i) 'The morality of acts committed in private.' In this sense to say that the law should not concern itself with matters of 'private morality' is simply to say that it should not interfere with acts committed in private. When Lord Devlin says that 'as far as possible privacy should be respected' it is privacy in this sense that he has in mind.

(ii) 'The morality of acts which have no tendency to injure others.' This seems to be the sense in which the Wolfenden Report uses the expression. Whether acts private in sense (i) are also necessarily private in sense (ii) is one of the main questions at issue.

(iii) 'The morality of acts whose performance is properly a matter for private judgement.' Thus Professor Hart in The Concept of Law (p. 179) speaks of private morality as 'shown in the individual's recognition of ideals which he need not either share with others or regard as a source of criticism of others, still less of society as a whole'. Professor Hart would, I think, hold that all actions, which have no tendency to hurt others are, if they are proper subjects of moral judgement at all, matters of 'private morality' in sense (iii). But it is a controversial question whether any morality is private in this sense.

which are above those of the law.'[30] This point is obvious but needs to be emphasized, because people often fail to distinguish the two questions posed earlier—the question of society's right to pass a moral judgement and the question whether the law should be used to enforce the judgement. These four principles are regarded by Lord Devlin not as hard and fast rules but as considerations which should be taken into account in answering the third of his questions. The error in the Wolfenden Report is that of looking for some single principle to explain the division between crime and sin.

The Report finds it in the principle that the criminal law exists for the protection of individuals; ... but the true principle is that the law exists for the protection of society. It does not discharge its function by protecting the individual from injury, annoyance, corruption and exploitation; the law must protect also the institutions and the community of ideas, political and moral, without which people cannot live together. Society cannot ignore the morality of the individual any more than it can his loyalty; it flourishes on both and without either it dies.[31]

I make no apology for this rather full summary of Lord Devlin's initial lecture, much of which has consisted of direct quotation. Since it has provoked an enormous amount of critical discussion, some of which we shall have to consider, it is important that the tone and balance as well as the leading themes of Lord Devlin's argument should be kept in mind.

Professor Hart's considered reply to Lord Devlin's thesis is to be found in three lectures delivered at Stanford University in 1962 and published under the title, *Law, Liberty and Morality*. Professor Hart's book contains also a critique of the views of the nineteenth-century jurist James Fitzjames Stephen, but I propose to concentrate on his criticisms of Lord Devlin and on the alternative answer which he proposes to Lord Devlin's question, which he (Professor Hart) formulates as follows: 'Is the fact that certain conduct is by common standards immoral sufficient to justify making that conduct punishable by law? It is morally permissible to enforce morality as such?'[32] This way of putting the question brings into relief two features of it: (a) It is a moral question as well as a question *about* morality. (b) It is a question of *justification*. Hence Lord Devlin's principle that a society may take the steps required to preserve its organized existence is to be understood as a principle of '*critical morality*', i.e. morality used in the criticism of social institutions as distinct from '*positive morality*', the morality actually accepted and shared by a given social group. To say that the legal enforcement of morality (or of anything else) requires justification is to imply that it is *prima facie* objectionable. Why is this? Professor Hart suggests two reasons. For those who offend it involves deprivation of liberty and infliction of pain; for those who are deterred from offending by fear of punishment, it imposes restrictions on liberty. Justification of legal enforcement is, then, required (a) because the unimpeded exercise of free choice is a value in itself, (b) because it is valuable to experiment—even with living, (c) for simpler utilitarian reasons, especially in sexual cases. 'For both the difficulties involved in the repression of sexual impulses and the consequences of repression are quite different from those involved in the abstention from "ordinary crime".'[33]

This is a piece of useful preliminary clarification, with the bulk of which Lord Devlin may be presumed to agree. The only statement with which he specifically expresses disagreement is (a) that the unimpeded exercise of free choice is a value in itself. 'Freedom', he says, 'is not a good thing in itself. We believe it to be good because out of freedom there comes more good than bad.' And he claims Mill's support: 'If a free society is better than a disciplined one, it is because—and this certainly was Mill's view—it is better for a man himself that he should be free to seek his own good in his own way and better too for the society to which he belongs, since thereby a way may be found to a greater good for all.'[34] But it is clear that he would attach less importance than Mill to (b) the value of experiments with living.[35] There are, as will become clear

[32] p. 4.   [33] p. 22.   [34] p. 108.   [35] See especially p. 107.

later, varieties of liberalism. But the natural starting point of
any contemporary discussion of liberalism is Mill's *Essay on
Liberty* and it is with Mill that Professor Hart begins, noting[36]
that the principles of the Wolfenden Committee are strikingly
like Mill's. Mill said, 'The only purpose for which power can
rightly be exercised over any member of a civilized community
against his will is to prevent harm to others. His own good
either physical or moral is not a sufficient warrant. He cannot
rightfully be compelled to do or forbear because it will be
better for him to do so, because it will make him happier, because in the opinion of others to do so would be wise or even
right.'[37] (This principle he would not apply to children or to
backward societies.)

Professor Hart does not propose to defend the whole of what
Mill said. He proceeds, indeed, to modify it considerably. But
he does take his stand with Mill on the question of the enforcement of morality. In so doing he has to define his position with
respect to Lord Devlin's contention that the criminal law of
England, as at present constituted, contains certain provisions
which can only be justified as seeking to enforce morality, so
that those who wish to follow Mill are committed to more or
less radical reform of the existing law. This he does in a
chapter on 'The Use and Abuse of Examples'.

He concedes straight away that both in England and
America the criminal law contains rules which *can* only be explained as attempts to enforce morality as such, mostly in the
realm of sexual morality. In England they include laws against
forms of homosexual behaviour between males, sodomy, best-
iality, incest, living on the earnings of prostitution, keeping a
house for prostitution, and also, since the decision in Shaw's
case, a conspiracy to corrupt public morals, interpreted to
mean, in substance, leading others (in the opinion of a jury)
'morally astray'. But there are other cases which in Professor
Hart's opinion are wrongly regarded as instances of the enforcement of morality. These are laws against abortion, against those
forms of bigamy or polygamy which do not involve decep-

[36] p. 14.   [37] *On Liberty*, p. 73 (Everyman Edition).

tion, against suicide and the practice of euthanasia. In America the penal codes of the various states list many more offences which can only be interpreted as attempts to enforce morality. About any laws which are *correctly* interpreted as attempts to enforce morality Professor Hart has no more to say. He agrees with Mill that they should cease to form part of the criminal law. But about the others, he maintains, 'We are not forced to choose between jettisoning them or assenting to the principle that the criminal law may be used for that purpose.'[38] For an alternative account can be given of them.

He turns, first of all, to Lord Devlin's treatment of the principle that the consent of the victim is not an admissible defence against a criminal charge. Lord Devlin argues that this principle can only be explained on the hypothesis that the law is concerned to enforce a moral principle, the sanctity of human life (and, Professor Hart adds, the physical integrity of the person). To this he objects that it is simply not true. 'The rules excluding the victim's consent as a defence to charges of murder or assault may perfectly well be explained as a piece of paternalism, designed to protect individuals against themselves. Mill no doubt might have protested against a paternalistic policy of using the law to protect even a consenting victim from bodily harm nearly as much as he protested against laws used merely to enforce positive morality; but this does not mean that these two policies are identical.' Indeed, 'Mill distinguishes "because it will be better for him" and "because it will make him happier" from "because in the opinion of others it would be right".'[39]

The distinction between 'paternalism' and 'the enforcement of morals' is of central importance in Professor Hart's position. Its introduction requires him to modify Mill's original principle substantially and enables him to drive a wedge deep into Lord Devlin's argument. But he devotes surprisingly little space to defining its terms, so that we are left in some doubt as to what are to count as cases of 'paternalism' and 'the enforcement of morals' respectively. Clearly his first task must be to

[38] p. 29.   [39] p. 31.

apply the distinction to Lord Devlin's original list and this he does somewhat incompletely, with a brief consideration of cruelty to animals and a careful examination of the law on bigamy. 'We are still left,' Lord Devlin subsequently complained, 'with five crimes about which Professor Hart says nothing.'[40] This is not strictly true, for of the five crimes Lord Devlin originally mentioned, euthanasia, suicide, duelling, abortion, and incest, one, incest, is included in Professor Hart's list of crimes explicable only as attempts to enforce morality and therefore on Professor Hart's principles should not be a crime at all. The remainder, it is implied, can be interpreted as pieces of paternalism. With duelling this is obviously the case. With regard to euthanasia, suicide, and abortion the case is not so clear. It requires further examination.

However, having, to his own satisfaction, knocked away the supports which Lord Devlin claimed to derive from the principles and practice of the existing criminal law, Professor Hart has still to meet his principal theoretical contention that 'society may use the law to preserve morality in the same way as it uses it to safeguard anything else that is essential to its existence'.[41] He undertakes this task in the third lecture on 'Varieties of Enforcement'. He points out, in the first instance, that one can distinguish a moderate and an extreme form of the thesis that the criminal law might justifiably be used to enforce morality. The moderate form of the thesis, which is the one Lord Devlin ostensibly adopts, is that a shared morality is the cement of society, so that the law may enforce morality as a means to an end. The extreme thesis (adopted by Stephen) is that the enforcement of morality is a good in itself even if immoral acts harm no one directly, or indirectly (by weakening the moral cement of society).

Lord Devlin, he says, certainly *appears* to adopt the moderate thesis, but whether he really does so is hard to tell because of the obscurity of his exposition. '... It is not at all clear that for him the statement that immorality jeopardizes or weakens

[40] p. 138.   [41] p. 11.

society is a statement of empirical fact. It seems sometimes to be an *a priori* assumption, and sometimes a necessary truth and a very odd one.'[42] The reason for thinking this is that Lord Devlin produces no *evidence* to show that 'deviation from accepted sexual morality, even by adults in private, is something which, like treason, threatens the existence of society. No reputable historian has maintained this thesis, and there is indeed much evidence against it.' 'Lord Devlin's belief in it, and his apparent indifference to the question of evidence, are at points traceable to an undiscussed assumption. This is that all morality—sexual morality together with the morality that forbids acts injurious to others such as killing, stealing, and dishonesty—forms a single seamless web, so that those who deviate from any part are likely or perhaps bound to deviate from the whole. It is of course clear (and one of the oldest insights of political theory) that society could not exist without a morality which mirrored and supplemented the law's proscription of conduct injurious to others. But there is again no evidence to support, and much to refute, the theory that those who deviate from conventional sexual morality are in other ways hostile to society.'[43]

There is no doubt, I think, that Lord Devlin's thesis *is* obscure at this point, which, since it is at the centre of his entire argument, requires very careful examination. It is important, however, to be clear just where Professor Hart is disagreeing with him, for in at least one important respect he seems to agree. 'It is, of course, clear ... that society could not exist without a morality.' If we ask whether *this* assertion, which Professor Hart himself makes, is *a priori* or empirical, it appears from what he goes on to say that he is inclined to regard it as *a priori*. For his next move is to accuse Lord Devlin of passing from 'the acceptable proposition that *some* shared morality is essential to the existence of any society to the unacceptable proposition that a society is identical with its morality as that is at any given moment of its history, so that a change in its morality is tantamount to the destruction of a society. The

[42] p. 50   [43] p. 51.

former proposition', he continues, 'might even be accepted as a necessary rather than an empirical truth depending on a quite plausible definition of society as a body of men who hold certain moral views in common. But the latter proposition is absurd.' Why is Lord Devlin supposed to hold this absurd opinion? Because 'It is only on this absurd criterion of what it is for the same society to continue to exist that it could be asserted without evidence that any deviation from a society's shared morality threatens its existence.'[44]

But if it *is* Lord Devlin's view that a society is to be identified with its morality, then he is, after all, an exponent of the extreme thesis. For he is saying that the enforcement of morality is an end in itself. Hence Professor Hart observes that 'Lord Devlin hovers somewhat ambiguously between one form of the extreme thesis and the moderate thesis.'

We shall need to look more closely at this later. Meanwhile it is worth noticing that the assertion that *some* shared morality is essential to the existence of any society is, taken by itself, ambiguous. It may mean either that there are certain moral principles (which could be listed) such that any society must recognize these principles in order to exist; or that any society in order to exist must have some shared moral principles (though not any particular ones). Professor Hart makes it clear that it is the former interpretation that he has in mind, for, as he says, 'society could not exist without a morality which mirrored and supplemented the law's proscription of conduct injurious to others'.

Whichever interpretation is adopted it is necessary to reckon with Lord Devlin's contention that 'society may use the law to preserve morality in the same way as it uses it to safeguard anything else that is essential to its existence'—not, indeed, the whole of its morality, but that part of it which, on either view, is essential to its existence. It looks as if Lord Devlin's argument might, even on Professor Hart's

[44] p. 52.

premises, sanction enforcement of *some* morality, though perhaps not 'private morality' (however that phrase is to be interpreted).

These are difficult questions, but on any showing they are central to this debate.

2

In what Sense is a Shared Morality
Essential for Society?

I ATTEMPTED in the first chapter a summary of the main points at issue between Lord Devlin and Professor Hart on the question of the enforcement of morals. Since both participants in this debate are recognizably liberals it may seem hard to account for the warmth of their disagreement. Surely there must be somewhere in the background more radical differences than have yet appeared? I am inclined to think there are, but I want to approach them by way of a discussion, as careful as I can make it, of the arguments each has put forward.

Lord Devlin began the debate by a critique of the principle adopted by the Wolfenden Committee, which was, as he noted, derived from Mill. Professor Hart, while prepared to modify Mill considerably, remains firmly on his side with respect to the particular issue upon which Lord Devlin attacked him, viz. the enforcement of morals. In the course of his criticism of Lord Devlin's Maccabaean Lecture Professor Hart accuses him of obscurity on the central point, although he is prepared to make some concessions to what, upon one interpretation at least, he seems to be saying. Now there is, I think, no doubt that Lord Devlin *is* obscure in what he has to say about the right of society to preserve its existence, although Professor Hart is, himself, not wholly clear in his comments upon it.

Lord Devlin argues that 'a recognized morality is as necessary to society as, say, a recognized government'; therefore 'society may use the law to preserve morality in the same way as it uses it to safeguard anything else that is essential to its existence'.[1] In a later lecture[2] he says, by way of illustration,

---

[1] p. 11.   [2] 'On Democracy and Morality', p. 90.

'[the law maker] has not to argue with himself about the merits of monogamy and polygamy; he has merely to observe that monogamy is an essential part of the structure of the society to which he belongs.... His mandate is to preserve the essentials of his society....' Elsewhere he lays down the principle 'There must be toleration of the maximum individual freedom that is consistent with the integrity of society.'[3]

Professor Hart complains that it is not clear whether the assertion that immorality jeopardizes or weakens society is intended as a statement of empirical fact or as a necessary truth. If it is intended as empirical it requires to be supported by evidence, which is not provided—and is not, in fact, to be had. He inclines to the view that Lord Devlin relies upon 'an undiscussed assumption ... that all morality—sexual morality together with the morality that forbids acts injurious to others, such as killing, stealing, and dishonesty—forms a single seamless web, so that those who deviate from any part are likely or perhaps bound to deviate from the whole'.[4] And he goes on to charge Lord Devlin with moving 'from the acceptable proposition that *some* shared morality is essential to the existence of any society to the unacceptable proposition that a society is identical with its morality as that is at any given moment of its history, so that a change in its morality is tantamount to the destruction of a society'. The former assertion may be a necessary truth, the latter is absurd, 'for it would prevent us saying that the morality of a given society had changed'.

Lord Devlin replies to this charge in a note which he has appended to his original lecture,[5]

I do not assert that *any* deviation from a society's shared morality threatens its existence any more than I assert that *any* subversive activity threatens its existence. I assert that they are both activities which are capable in their nature of threatening the existence of society so that neither can be put beyond the law.…

The proposition that I make in the text is that if (as I understand Professor Hart to agree, at any rate for the purposes of the argument) you cannot have a society without morality, the law

<hr />

[3] p. 16.   [4] p. 51.   [5] p. 13 n.

can be used to enforce morality as something that is essential to a society. I cannot see why this proposition (whether it is right or wrong) should mean that morality can never be changed without the destruction of society. If morality is changed, the law can be changed.

From this I think it is clear that Lord Devlin does *not* hold that a society is identified with its entire morality at a given time. He is *not* maintaining that any change in its morality is destructive of it in this trivial sense. What he *is* maintaining is that there are no types of immorality which are in their nature incapable of threatening the existence of society, so that they can safely be regarded as 'not the law's business'. However, it still remains obscure what 'threatening society's existence' means. 'If a quarter or half the population got drunk every night,' Lord Devlin asks, 'what sort of society would it be?' He does not answer the question, but we are, I think, to understand that its existence would have been threatened, its integrity compromised. But what would this amount to? There is no reason to suppose that, in any straightforward sense, it would have been destroyed. It would presumably continue to exist but in a rather worse condition than before. 'Worse' in what sense? Should we say that it was 'weakened' or 'corrupted'? Are we judging it from a pragmatic or from a moral point of view?

In a later passage[6] Lord Devlin indicates that his criterion is not a moral one.

'It is generally accepted that some shared morality, that is, some common agreement about what is right and wrong, is an essential element in the constitution of any society. Without it there would be no cohesion. But polygamy can be as cohesive as monogamy and I am prepared to believe that a society based on free love and a community of children could be just as strong (though according to our ideas it could not be as good) as one based on the family. What is important is not the quality of the creed but the strength of the belief in it. . . . On this reasoning there is nothing inherently objectionable in the change of an old morality for a new one. Why then is the law used to guard existing moral beliefs? It is because an old morality cannot be changed

[6] pp. 114–15.

for a new morality as an old coat for a new one. The old belief must be driven out by disbelief. Polygamy could not be established in England or in the United States unless there was first created a disbelief in the value of monogamy. If change is in progress there will for a long period be no common belief in the value of either institution.... But no-one, it will be said, wants to subvert a whole morality. All that is sought is freedom to make peripheral changes or, if not quite peripheral, changes that will leave the bulk of morality intact; nothing will be done that will seriously diminish the cohesive force of a common morality.

The difficulty is, Lord Devlin goes on to argue, that

most men take their morality as a whole and in fact derive it, though this is irrelevant, from some religious doctrine. To destroy the belief in one part of it will probably result in weakening the belief in the whole. Professor Hart says that to argue in this way is to treat morality as if it 'forms a single seamless web'. Seamlessness presses the simile rather hard, but apart from that, I should say that for most people morality is a web of beliefs rather than a number of unconnected ones.

In this passage Lord Devlin seems quite happy about a change in a society's morality, so long as the pace of change is regulated, so that at any given point in its history *belief* in what happens at that time to be its morality is adequately strong. The quality of the morality is irrelevant. 'Bad societies can live on bad morals just as well as good societies on good ones.'[7]

It seems to follow that the sense in which the society in which a quarter of the people got drunk every night would have been weakened, is not that it would have become morally corrupt. In what sense then? The obvious alternative is the utilitarian one: people who got drunk every night would be less efficient, less reliable, and the community in general less happy. This is the sort of society it would be.

The later passage with its emphasis upon the cohesive force of shared moral *beliefs* seems at first sight to have in mind an altogether different concept of the preservation of a society. What exactly is it that is threatened if people cease to believe

[7] p. 94.

in the old code before they have come to believe in the new one? The suggestion seems to be that, because of people's tendency to swallow their morality whole, belief in the entire existing code will in fact be weakened. (To this extent Lord Devlin accepts the 'seamless web' doctrine.) But why should this matter? Because 'it is generally accepted that some shared morality, that is, some common agreement about what is right and wrong, is an essential element in the constitution of any society. Without it there would be no cohesion.' So the argument would seem to be this. We do not know just how much cohesion is necessary for a society to exist, but we know that some cohesion is necessary. Some degree of shared morality is essential to this minimum of cohesion, and any weakening of moral belief may reduce it below this minimum; hence we cannot bind ourselves not to use the law to safeguard existing moral beliefs, no matter how peripheral they may appear to be.

The argument starts from a premise which is taken to be generally accepted and a form of which Professor Hart does, indeed, accept. As we saw, he is inclined to regard it as a necessary truth that some shared morality is essential to the existence of any society. But, as we also noticed, this statement is ambiguous. It may mean that there are certain moral principles (which could, in principle, be listed) such that any society, in order to survive, must recognize them. Or it may mean that any society, in order to exist, i.e. in order to be a society at all, must have some shared moral principles (though not any particular ones). I think that there is no doubt that Lord Devlin intends the latter interpretation; whereas Professor Hart intends the former. If there is this difference of interpretation it could explain how they succeed in deriving different conclusions from what is ostensibly the same premise. Professor Hart develops the former interpretation in his book *The Concept of Law*[8] under the heading, 'The Minimum Content of Natural Law'. He argues that

reflection on some very obvious generalisations—indeed truisms— concerning human nature and the world in which men live, shows

[8] p. 188.

that as long as these hold good, there are certain rules of conduct which any social organisation must contain if it is to be viable. Such rules do in fact constitute a common element in the law and conventional morality of all societies which have progressed to the point where these are distinguished as different forms of social control. With them are found, both in law and morals, much that is peculiar to a particular society and much that may seem arbitrary or a mere matter of choice.

We have already seen, in an earlier quotation from Professor Hart, what sort of rules these would be. It is the morality that condemns acts injurious to others which is necessary to the survival of *any* society. Indeed Professor Hart makes this explicit in *Law, Liberty and Morality*,[9] where he refers to 'the truth that since all social moralities, whatever else they may contain, make provision in some degree for such universal values as individual freedom, safety of life, and protection from deliberately inflicted harm, there will always be much in social morality that is worth preserving even at the cost in terms of these same values which legal enforcement involves'. And later: 'We should with Mill be alive to the truth that though these essential universal values must be secured, society can not only survive individual divergences in other fields from its prevalent morality, but profit from them.'[10]

These 'universal values' provide the basis for the 'critical morality' underlying Professor Hart's conception of the function of law, which is the same as that of the Wolfenden Committee 'to preserve public order and decency, to protect the citizens from what is offensive or injurious'. And Lord Devlin correctly interprets this position when he writes: 'The criminal law in carrying out these objects will undoubtedly overlap the moral law. Crimes of violence are morally wrong and they are also offences against good order; therefore they offend against both laws. But this is simply because the two laws in pursuit of different objectives happen to cover the same area. Such is the argument.'[11] It is clear from what Professor Hart says here and elsewhere that he regards sexual morality as on a totally

[9] p. 70. [10] p. 71. [11] p. 5.

C

different footing. In conceding the possibility (though not the plausibility) of certain critical moralities other than his own he writes: 'No doubt a critical morality based on the theory that all social morality had the status of divine commands or of eternal truth discovered by reason would not for obvious reasons now seem plausible. It is perhaps least plausible in relation to sexual morals, *determined as these so obviously are by variable tastes and conventions*' (my italics).[12]

It is now, I think, clear in what sense Professor Hart accepts the assertion that 'a shared morality is necessary to the existence of any society' and why he does not regard it as committing him in any degree to Lord Devlin's thesis about the enforcement of morals. There are, he believes, certain 'universal values' whose acceptance is necessary to the survival of any society, these being the utilitarian values upon which Bentham's and Mill's doctrine of the function of the law is based. The sexual morality of a society is not among these universal values and there is no reason to suppose that a change in sexual morality would have any repercussions upon them.

It looks then as if there are, as we suspected, considerable divergences between Lord Devlin and his opponents about the nature and scope of morality and this will become even more noticeable when we turn from Professor Hart to some of Lord Devlin's other critics. Before doing this, however, I want to return once again to what *Lord Devlin* meant by the assertion that a shared morality is necessary to the existence of a society. As we have seen, in the extended passage in the lecture 'On Mill and Morality'[13] the emphasis is entirely on the importance of shared *beliefs* as to what is right and wrong; there is no mention of the role of actions as distinct from beliefs, whereas in considering the hypothetical case of the spread of drunkenness to a quarter or half of the population it is the consequences of these people actually getting drunk that worry him, not of their changing their moral attitude to drunkenness. However, these differences of emphasis are not significant. A great deal of philosophical ingenuity has been exercised on

[12] p. 73.   [13] pp. 114–15.

the question whether a man can properly be said to believe that he ought not to do something and yet do it—believe that he ought not to get drunk and yet get drunk—but there would be general agreement that moral beliefs could not exist as moral beliefs unless 'normally and other things being equal' people abstained from doing what they believed to be wrong.

More interesting, however, is the fact that in this passage there is no suggestion that some moral beliefs may be more *important* than others (nothing like Professor Hart's stress upon 'universal values'). The impression is certainly created that all moral beliefs contribute equally to the stability of society. But in his references to monogamy a judgement of importance *is* implied. '[The law maker] has not to argue with himself about the merits of monogamy and polygamy; he has merely to observe that monogamy is an essential part of the structure of the society to which he belongs.... His mandate is to preserve *the essentials* of his society' (my italics).[14]

In talking in this way of the essentials of *his* society (my italics) Lord Devlin introduces a consideration that is largely absent from Professor Hart's discussion. The 'shared morality' to which Professor Hart was prepared to attach importance was a morality of 'universal values' which are, *ex hypothesi*, respected to a greater or lesser extent in any society, since no society is viable without them. Sexual morality was expressly excepted. Lord Devlin, while prepared to allow that polygamy may afford a perfectly adequate basis for a secure society, insists nevertheless that the law may properly be used to enforce monogamy in our society, as being among its essential institutions. In calling monogamy 'essential' to our society he is, presumably, calling attention to the ramifications of the institution of marriage, its relations to the institutions of parenthood and property, for example, which are so complex that, as Professor Toulmin observes, there is no question of our trying to replace Christian marriage by Muslim marriage.[15] It is obvious that a great deal of our sexual morality is intimately bound up with the institution of monogamous mar-

---

[14] p. 90.   [15] *The Place of Reason in Ethics*, p. 152.

riage, so that if Lord Devlin is right in holding that the law
has a proper concern with monogamy, it is at least plausible
to suggest that it cannot wholly disinterest itself in sexual
morality. Thus Lord Devlin writes,

> The institution of marriage is a good example for my purpose
> because it bridges the division, if there is one, between politics and
> morals. Marriage is part of the structure of our society and it is
> also the basis of a moral code which condemns fornication and
> adultery. The institution of marriage would be gravely threatened
> if individual judgements were permitted about the morality of
> adultery; on these points there must be a public morality.[16]

He goes on to say,

> People do not think of monogamy as something which has to be
> supported because our society has chosen to organize itself upon
> it; they think of it as something that is good in itself and offering
> a good way of life and that it is for that reason that our society
> has adopted it. I return to the statement ... that society means a
> community of ideas; without shared ideas on politics, morals, and
> ethics no society can exist.

At first sight this seems inconsistent with Lord Devlin's
earlier insistence that the *quality* of a society's morality does
not matter—'polygamy can be as cohesive as monogamy'—but
his point here is, presumably, that for an institution to work
there must be a belief in its value; whether this belief is justified does not, however, matter so far as its cohesive force is
concerned.

The importance of the issue of polygamy as a test of Professor Hart's thesis has been urged by Dean Rostow.[17] This
issue is one that has actually been adjudicated by the United
States Supreme Court, which, as Dean Rostow points out, 'has
upheld such laws, [against polygamy] in the teeth of the Constitutional provision that "Congress shall make no law respect-
ing an establishment of religion, or prohibiting the free
exercise thereof" '.[18]

[16] p. 9.
[17] *Cambridge Law Journal*, November 1960. Reprinted in *The Sovereign Prerogative*, Yale University Press, 1962.
[18] p. 191. See *Reynolds* v. *U.S.*, 98. U.S. 145 (1878) *Musser* v. *Utah*, 333. U.S.
95 (1948).

Should we ask [he says] whether the preference of the common morality in the United States for monogamy, enforced by the criminal law, is based on 'ignorance, superstition, or misunderstanding'? Does it derive from a 'false conception' that those who practise polygamy 'are in other ways dangerous or hostile to society'? Should we inquire whether polygamy is tolerable if confined, but 'gravely injurious' if allowed to spread? ... Suppose we engaged in all these acts of critical scrutiny and rational investigation which to my mind both the Professor and the Judge enjoin. Should we not then conclude that *monogamy is so fundamental a theme in the existing common morality of the United States* [my italics], that the condemnation of polygamy as a crime is justified, even though in the end the repugnance to it rests on 'feeling' and not on 'reason'?[19]

The reaction of Lord Devlin's opponents to this challenge is extremely interesting. Professor Hart deals with it in his book under the heading 'Private Immorality and Public Indecency'. Mr. Graham Hughes also examines it in his article on 'Morals and the Criminal Law'.[20] Both writers say little about polygamy and concentrate their attention on the crime of bigamy, perhaps because Mormonism has not yet made polygamy a live issue in this country as it was in the United States. This is a pity because bigamy, unlike polygamy, is not normally offered as an alternative social institution. The typical bigamist is a man who wants to evade his obligations to one wife rather than to assume responsibility for more than one. Hence it is far from obvious that a treatment of bigamy as prohibited by law in this country would be adequate to account for the proscription of polygamy in the United States.

The laws against polygamy and bigamy are instanced by Lord Devlin and Dean Rostow as cases of the enforcement of morals. The choice before their opponents would seem to be, therefore, (a) to deny that they ought to be prohibited by law, (b) to accept the prohibition, but deny that it is properly understood as exemplifying the enforcement of morals. Both Professor Hart and Mr. Hughes adopt the second course, though the rationale they actually discover for making bigamy a crime is in fact somewhat different. Professor Hart points

[19] p. 190   [20] *Yale Law Journal*, 1961, vol. 71 (i), pp. 662 ff.

out[21] that it is an offence in this country for a married person
to go through a ceremony of marriage with another, even if
the other knows of the existing marriage. Sexual cohabitation
with someone other than the spouse is not an offence and the
man may pose as married, so long as he does not go through a
ceremony. 'Why then,' he asks, 'does the law interfere at this
point, leaving the substantial immorality of sexual cohabitation alone?' He considers and dismisses as possible reasons for
the attitude of the law the public affront to the first spouse and
the risk of desertion and non-support, and inclines to the view
that the intention is 'to protect religious feelings from offence
by a public act desecrating the ceremony'.[22] 'If so,' he argues,
'it is important to see ... that the bigamist is punished neither
as irreligious nor as immoral but as a nuisance. For the law is
then concerned with the offensiveness to others of his public
conduct ... not with the immorality of his private conduct.'
He takes the case of bigamy to illustrate an important distinction, which he proceeds to elaborate, between the immorality
of a practice and its aspect as a public offensive act or nuisance.
To this we shall return later. Mr. Hughes finds a different basis
for the law on bigamy. After noting that the relation of monogamy to the law is very complex he continues,

> Monogamy is thus only protected by the criminal law to a
> limited extent, and what is ensured and protected is not the in-
> dissoluble sexual union of one man and one woman but rather a
> form of registration entailing certain legal consequences which
> again can be dissolved in certain eventualities. It is thus quite
> possible to conclude that the criminal prohibition of bigamy is or
> ought to be aimed at suppressing two evils: (1) the procurement
> of sexual relations by fraud, and (2) the confusion of a public
> system of registration on which a host of rights, duties, powers
> and privileges depends.... Making bigamy a crime is thus just as
> defensible on utilitarian grounds as is making a crime of rape or
> voting twice.[23]

What one notices at once about both these defences of the
existing practice is that they take entirely for granted that the
norm of marriage in this country is and ought to be monogamy.

[21] pp. 38 ff.   [22] p. 41.   [23] p. 674.

Given that this is the case it is, of course, true that confusion will result if people go through a marriage ceremony which the law holds invalid. It is also true that unscrupulous people may seek to procure sexual relations fraudulently by going through a second ceremony of marriage (though there are nowadays many easier ways of doing it). But all this has no bearing at all on the prior question why the law in this country does not allow people to contract *valid* bigamous or polygamous marriages if they want to. Why, for that matter, does not or should not the law recognize valid homosexual 'marriages'? It is because *this* question was clearly faced that the American decision on polygamy is of greater interest for this discussion than the English law on bigamy. For the United States Supreme Court was concerned explicitly with the question of *recognizing* polygamous marriages. To suggest, as Professor Hart does with reference to bigamy—as I have noted, he neglects the case of polygamy in the United States—that it is punished as an offence to the susceptibilities of the devout is to evade the entire weight of Dean Rostow's argument. The case is put forcefully by Lord Devlin himself,

Whether a man should be allowed to take more than one wife is something about which every society has to make up its mind one way or the other. In England we believe in the Christian idea of marriage and therefore adopt monogamy as a moral principle. Consequently the Christian institution of marriage has become the basis of family life and so part of the structure of our society. It is there not because it is Christian. It has got there because it is Christian, but it remains there because it is built into the house in which we live and could not be removed without bringing it down. The great majority of those who live in this country accept it because it is the Christian idea of marriage and for them the only true one. But a non-Christian is bound by it, not because it is part of Christianity but because, rightly or wrongly, it has been adopted by the society in which he lives.[24]

Lord Devlin says that this is a matter about which every society has to make up its mind one way or the other. In point of fact there is a third way. The law might recognize a plurality of valid forms of marriage (as indeed Lord Devlin himself

[24] p. 9.

suggests in his essay on *Morals and the Law of Marriage*).[25] The case against restriction is put by Glanville Williams, *Criminal Law* (second edition), p. 750:

The problem of conscience arises also with regard to the marriage laws. American courts refused to allow Mormons to practise polygamy for religious reasons as a minority sect, and English courts would act likewise. Yet the English allow polygamy in overseas territories of the Crown—where the strongly objectionable practices of slavery, suttee, and torture are forbidden. It would seem to be in keeping with the libertarian principles of a mature civilization to regard the polygamous practices of religious sects as merely an idiosyncrasy. If it is thought that the law should discountenance them, this may be done sufficiently by failure to provide for them in the civil law, rather than by attempting the sterner dissuasion of penal sanctions.

The point is, however, that the law has to take *some* stand on the matter. No society is content to allow relations between the sexes to be entirely a matter of individual preference. And if a society chooses to insist on a single pattern, it is difficult to believe that it is *eo ipso* guilty of unwarrantable interference with the freedom of its members.

Thus it seems to me that Devlin is right in holding that the law may take the line that monogamy as an institution is essential to our society and be justified in taking it. This does not mean that monogamy is essential to *any* society—obviously it is not. Nor does it mean that the law can never, or ought never, to alter on this point. It means simply that at any given period the law on marriage must be definite and that change, if it comes, must come slowly and must result in a law which, though different, is equally definite.

There are two important questions which now arise. (i) Is the law's protection of monogamy really a case of the enforcement of morals; or is Mr. Hughes right in maintaining that it is explicable simply as a pragmatic device in purely utilitarian terms? (ii) Given that the possibility of change is recognized what considerations should determine the direction of change? But before considering them we need to look a little further

[25] ch. IV.

into the question of what is involved in this notion of 'preserving the essentials of our society'.

The suggestion is that the law may be used to protect the essential institutions of a society, even though such institutions are not necessary to the survival of any society. We need to ask what is meant by calling an institution 'essential to a given society', and also what is involved in 'protecting' it. Professor Hart argues that there are only two senses in which an institution can be said to be essential to a society. Either it is such that without it the society could not survive as a society; or it is such (and this will be true of any institution, however peripheral), that without it the society would be different. Thus monogamy is not essential in the first sense, for our society would not disintegrate if it became polygamous. It is, of course, essential in the second sense, but this is entirely trivial. Hence he accuses Lord Devlin of holding that 'a change in its morality is tantamount to the destruction of a society', and characterizes this proposition as absurd.

To this Lord Devlin might well reply that to call an institution 'essential' is to imply that, without it, the society would not only be different, but different in some fundamental way. The point can be illustrated from the Franks Report on Oxford University, in particular its remarks on the collegiate structure of the university and the tutorial system, and the relationship between them. Thus the Commission write (para. 209)

Inside the college the social and administrative arrangements, the Common Table and the service in college government, make a special way of life. This college life, involving daily preoccupation with the problems and aspirations of the young, has had the effect of concentrating the interest of senior members of Oxford on the teaching of undergraduates. It has also ... been responsible for the strength of the democratic spirit in the University. The absence of hierarchical structure in the organization of the work, the freedom of initiative, both in teaching and research, enjoyed by the fellows of small self-governing communities, these are benefits which Oxford derives from its traditional multicellular pattern. An overwhelming majority of our witnesses, both inside and outside Oxford, believed that these features of the system should be safeguarded. We emphatically agree with these witnesses.

The Commission note (para. 216) that 'in building up this way of life the tutorial plays an important part' and they go on to assess the educational merits of the system, expressing their belief 'that the tutorial should continue to be the characteristic feature of Oxford's system and that the tutorial should continue to be firmly rooted in the colleges. We intend that reading and writing, rather than listening, should continue to be the salient characteristics of the Oxford system.' (para. 240.) Finally they consider the pattern of the Oxford courses, the Final Honour Schools, as designed to provide 'education in depth', and conclude, 'We believe that education in this sense is most valuable and should be maintained whatever changes are made in the syllabus. It is not of course the only method by which young men and women may be trained to think. But it is an effective method, it is suited to the tutorial system and it is one in which this University is experienced. We think therefore that it is in the national interest to retain this method in Oxford.' (para. 245.)

The Commission have selected certain institutions as of such central importance to the University that they should be preserved. They are not saying 'Without these institutions Oxford would cease to exist as a university', nor are they saying 'Without these institutions Oxford would be a different sort of university'. They are not even saying, simply, 'Without them Oxford would be a worse university'. They are saying something more like 'Without them Oxford would lack its characteristic excellences'. Other universities, they would concede, have their own virtues, but the distinctive merits of Oxford are bound up with *these* institutions.

It may be objected that if 'essential to a given society' is taken to mean 'essential to its form of life', as this illustration suggests, this is a sense quite different from that of 'essential to cohesion', which is what Lord Devlin appears to have in mind. Whether this is so must wait upon more careful consideration of Lord Devlin's position. But it is evident, even at first sight, that the two senses are not wholly unrelated. It is true that a society will not entirely disintegrate if its institutions are dissolved or weakened. It may well possess enough 'cohesion' to survive and perhaps to do so without difficulty. Nevertheless what makes institutions fundamental is, presumably, that they satisfy certain important human needs in a systematic manner which is generally thought to be valuable. Characteristically they interlock with other institutions satisfying other needs. Institutions, so understood, are essential to people's living together in a satisfactory fashion and so contribute to 'cohesion'. The role of institutions in securing 'cohesion' is well described by Professor Dorothy Emmet.

In a social environment, each individual is set in multiple criss-crossing relationships, so that the results of his actions affect and are affected by those of other people, producing snowballing effects (such as inflationary spirals which no one has intended, though they can be understood and controlled through Keynesian economic techniques). Also the frameworks of actions are established patterns of social relationships and ways of doing things— institutions, in fact—which produce situations in which some kinds of action can be effective and other kinds discouraged or rendered ineffective. In a chaotic aggregate of individuals few purposes could be effective (the Hobbesian insight). Sociological analysis shows why some kinds of purpose are likely to be pursued effectively under some forms of social relationship and others not.[26]

Institutions, therefore, play an essential part in enabling people to live together and a satisfactory society will be one which has learnt how to protect its institutions without at the same time securing them altogether against change or criticism.

As we have seen Lord Devlin is not concerned with the *merits* of the institutions which are to be preserved. It is enough for him that they are, as a matter of fact, fundamental institutions in our society; though, if they are to have cohesive power, it is important that people should *believe* in their value. The individual who does not believe in their value is to be told that 'if he wants to live in the house, he must accept it as

[26] *Rules, Roles and Relations*, p. 125.

built in the way in which it is'.[27] This apparent indifference to
the value, as distinct from the effectiveness, of institutions, is a
defect in Lord Devlin's position which his critics have been
quick to notice. In point of fact it sometimes happens that an
effort is made by law to safeguard institutions less because they
are thought to be good than because they are thought to be
characteristic. No doubt in all such cases motives are mixed,
but it is reasonable to suspect that some of those who want to
preserve the Welsh language and the Welsh Sunday do so not
because they believe that these institutions have peculiar
merits but because they are characteristically Welsh. They
want to preserve the *Welshness* of Wales, even if it means that
the majority have to learn a minority language and those who
want to drink on Sundays are frustrated. This derives perhaps
from a romantic conception of nationality, a diluted residue
of which is to be found in talk about 'The British Way of
Life'. The fact that this conception is capable of such grave
corruptions as the *Herrenvolk* doctrine of Nazi Germany or
South African apartheid does not mean that it has no proper
place in our thinking about society. It is, indeed, a simple
extension to nations or other cultural groups of the principle
to which Mill attached so much importance in relation to
individuals, 'there is no reason that all human existence
should be constructed on some one or some small number of
patterns'.[28]

If there is any value in diversity, it may require active preservation at a time when commercial pressures tend strongly
towards cultural uniformity. So the question is worth asking
whether the use of the law for such a purpose is justifiable and
if so, on what grounds. It could not be on the ground that these
are universal values necessary to the survival of any society.
Nor could it be on the ground that the society in question
would otherwise experience the sort of social chaos that might
be expected to result from the collapse of the institution of
marriage. Without the Welsh language and the Welsh Sunday
Wales would suffer no greater injury than that of becoming

[27] p. 9.   [28] *On Liberty*, p. 125 (Everyman Edition).

largely indistinguishable from England. One would have to say something like that the survival of the Welsh way of life was at stake, not what makes Wales viable, or what makes it civilised, but what makes it Welsh.

Lord Devlin wishes to use the law to 'preserve' or 'protect' the essentials of our society and this conception also needs to be clarified. For there are ways of doing this which fall short of enforcement by the criminal law. It might be possible, as Dr. Glanville Williams suggests, to discountenance polygamous practices sufficiently 'by failure to provide for them in the civil law rather than by attempting the sterner dissuasion of penal sanctions'.[29] It is one thing to grant legal recognition only to monogamous marriages; another to make bigamy or polygamy punishable offences. Hence opponents of Lord Devlin might occupy one of two positions. They might take the extreme position that the law should not identify itself with any but Professor Hart's 'universal values' or the more moderate position (which appears to be that of Professor Hart himself) that, although the law may recognize a morality which goes beyond them, it should not enforce it by penal sanctions. The latter position would seem to imply either that such sanctions could never be needed, or that the importance of the institutions to be protected could never be great enough to justify them.

Enough has been said to show that the conception of 'preserving the existence of a society' or of 'preserving its essentials' is far from simple and that it is not exhausted by the alternatives of 'preserving those universal values which are necessary to *any* society' or 'preserving intact a society's entire morality at any given moment' which are all that Professor Hart seems prepared to recognize. So Lord Devlin cannot be impaled on the dilemma that his thesis is either an absurd would-be necessary truth or a totally unsupported factual statement.

It is, therefore, worth while persevering with his argument.

[29] *Criminal Law* (second edition), p. 750.

3

'The Man in the Clapham Omnibus': Democracy and Morality

LORD DEVLIN asked three questions:[1]

(1) Has society the right to pass judgement at all on matters of morals? Ought there, in other words, to be a public morality or are morals always a matter for private judgement?

(2) If society has the right to pass judgement has it also the right to use the weapon of the law to enforce it?

(3) If so, ought it to use that weapon in all cases or only in some; and if only in some, on what principles should it distinguish?

He answers the first two questions by putting forward his central thesis:

If society has a right to make a judgement and has it on the basis that a recognized morality is as necessary to society as, say, a recognized government, then society may use the law to preserve morality in the same way as it uses it to safeguard anything else that is essential to its existence.[2]

We have spent some time examining this conception of a shared morality as essential to the existence of a society and have seen that it cannot be dismissed out of hand. Professor Hart and Lord Devlin agree that there are some moral principles whose acceptance is necessary to the survival of any society. For Professor Hart these are the principles which forbid injury to others and in his view these 'universal values' are the only ones the law has a right to protect. But Lord Devlin argues, I think convincingly, that every state protects certain institutions which are thought to be essential to that particular

[1] p. 7.　　　　　　[2] p. 11.

society, although they are not essential to any society whatever. He instances the institution of monogamous marriage in this country and the United States. So legislation to recognize and protect monogamous marriage is intended, in an intelligible sense, to protect one of the essentials of our society. If, for the sake of argument, this contention is accepted, Lord Devlin's third question arises. However, before going into this question Lord Devlin in his original lecture addressed himself to the problem of ascertaining the moral judgements of society. What *is* the morality which society has a *prima facie* right to enforce? He answers that 'immorality ... for the purpose of the law is what every right-minded person is presumed to consider to be immoral'. The reasonable or right-minded man is 'the man in the Clapham omnibus' or 'the man in the jury box'. 'For the moral judgement of society must be something about which any twelve men or women drawn at random might after discussion be expected to be unanimous.'[3]

Having said this he proceeds to answer the third question by laying down four principles to guide legislators in discriminating between those moral offences which should be prohibited by law and those which should not. These four principles are recognizably liberal in tone. There must be toleration of the maximum individual freedom that is consistent with the integrity of society. It must be recognized that the limits of tolerance shift. As far as possible privacy should be respected. The law is concerned with a minimum and not with a maximum standard of behaviour. Nevertheless they have done little to mollify Lord Devlin's critics. 'These reservations,' says Mr. Hughes,[4] 'although they appear to temper the severity of Lord Devlin's approach, are not finally reassuring, for we are offered no guide as to their comparative importance when set beside the reprobation of the "right-minded person".'

The passage to which the greatest exception has been taken occurs as a gloss upon the first principle. 'Nothing,' says Lord Devlin, 'should be punished by the law that does not lie beyond the limits of tolerance. It is not nearly enough to say that the

[3] p. 15.   [4] p. 678.

majority dislike a practice; there must be a real feeling of reprobation. Those who are dissatisfied with the present law on homosexuality often say that the opponents of reform are swayed simply by disgust. If that were so it would be wrong, but I do not think one can ignore disgust if it is deeply felt and not manufactured. Its presence is a good indication that the bounds of toleration are being reached. Not everything is to be tolerated. No society can do without intolerance, indignation and disgust; they are the forces behind the moral law....'[5] Lord Devlin cites as an example the disgust felt at cruelty to animals.

The line Lord Devlin takes here is at any rate consistent. The morality the law is concerned with is the *de facto* 'positive morality' of the society in question, since what matters is its cohesive power and not its acceptability on other grounds. Feelings of reprobation and disgust are of significance as indicating that the limits of toleration are being reached, i.e. that the point has come when the integrity of society is being threatened. He insists that the passage should be read 'in subjection to the statement that the judgement which the community passes on a practice must be calm and dispassionate and that mere disapproval is not enough to justify interference'.[6] Thus about homosexuality he says: 'we should ask ourselves in the first instance whether, looking at it calmly and dispassionately, we regard it as a vice so abominable that its mere presence is an offence. If that is the genuine feeling of the society in which we live I do not see how society can be denied the right to eradicate it.'[7]

The language and the argument of these passages have driven Lord Devlin's critics to charge him with irrationalism. 'Here,' says Mr. Hughes, 'is an overt rejection of rationality startling in its frankness,'[8] while Professor Wollheim accuses him of adopting a theory of society which is 'totally irrationalist' and excludes 'what it has been the triumph of civilization to establish: the taming of conscience by reason'.[9] But not all

[5] p. 17.   [6] p. ix.   [7] p. 17.   [8] p. 675.
[9] 'Crime, Sin and Mr. Justice Devlin', *Encounter*, November 1959, p. 39.

readers interpret him so. Dean Rostow says, 'Nothing in Lord Devlin's lecture would weaken the primary importance of detached and dispassionate scholarship, conducted at the highest level of reasonableness we can attain, in the work of social reform and the reform of the law.'[10]

Oddly enough, in spite of Lord Devlin's clarity of style, it is by no means easy to discover exactly where he stands on this issue. However, one must be careful to examine his argument without being swayed by a purely emotional reaction to the language he uses. 'It is not easy to see,' says Mr. Hughes, 'how a judgement that uses terms such as "abominable vice" can be made "calmly and dispassionately".'[11] No doubt the language is old-fashioned, but it is hard to believe that there are no forms of evil conduct that in Mr. Hughes' view a reasonable man would on reflection consider to be detestable. Nevertheless Mr. Hughes' criticism is more substantial than would appear from this momentary lapse. He is concerned with Lord Devlin's apparent indifference to the rational basis of reprobation and disgust, as contrasted with the Benthamite tradition.

The Benthamite method compels us to do our best to express our disgust in the language of values. The value here advanced [in the case of cruelty to animals] is that the infliction of suffering on any sensate creature is to be deplored and prohibited, unless there are very compelling reasons that outbalance this value (as in the case of vivisection). If we pursue this rigorous method into the example of homosexual behaviour, it can be seen that the reaction of disgust which it is alleged is felt by the majority of right-thinking men is much less easy to state in the form of a defensible value judgement. Here the disgust is perhaps more akin to the disgust which some people may feel about gluttony or snoring, or wearing gaudy ties. One cannot help suspecting that the morality of an established caste is being too uninquiringly preferred as the morality of the right-thinking majority....[12]

Here Mr. Hughes is, apparently, quite prepared to grant that disgust may be rational; he simply questions whether disgust at homosexual behaviour *is* rational, and suspects that

[10] p. 196.   [11] p. 678.   [12] p. 676.

D

it is not. He shares, in fact, Professor Hart's convictions about
the largely irrational character of conventional sexual morality.
It would be interesting to explore the rational basis upon
which gluttony and snoring are held, apparently, to be morally
equivalent, but it would be irrelevant. The question at issue
is not whether Lord Devlin's morality or Mr. Hughes' is
rationally defensible but whether Lord Devlin is, as his critics
allege, indifferent to the rationality or otherwise of the common morality which he is prepared in principle to have enforced by law.

Lord Devlin considers this criticism in a lecture on 'Democracy and Morality'.[13] He takes his start once again from the
familiar contention that society may legislate to preserve itself.
Hence the law maker has to enforce those ideas about right and
wrong which are already accepted by the society for which he
is legislating. 'His mandate is to preserve the essentials of his
society, not to reconstruct them according to his own ideas.'[14]
So 'he is concerned with what is acceptable to the ordinary
man, the man in the jury box, who might also be called the
reasonable man or the right-minded man'. One of the points
which is emphasized by calling him the man in the jury box
is that 'the man in the jury box does not give a snap judgement
but returns his verdict after argument, instruction, and deliberation'.

Lord Devlin now turns to the reaction of many philosophers
and academic lawyers to this doctrine. 'They dislike it very
much. It reduces morality, they feel, to the level of a question
of fact. What Professor H. L. A. Hart calls rationalist
morality,[15] which I take to be morality embodied in the
rational judgement of men who have studied moral questions
and pondered long on what the answers ought to be, will be
blown aside by a gust of popular morality compounded of all
the irrational prejudices and emotions of the man in the street.
Societies in the past have tolerated witch-hunting and burnt
heretics: was that done in the name of morality? There are

[13] ch. V.   [14] p. 90.
[15] 'Immorality and Treason', *Listener*, 30 July 1959, vol. 62, pp. 162, 163.

societies today whose moral standards permit them to discriminate against men because of their colour: have we to accept them? Is reason to play no part in the separation of right from wrong?'[16]

Lord Devlin observes that in a democracy we have no hesitation in allowing important political questions to be settled in accordance with the opinion of the ordinary citizen. The fact that we feel otherwise about a pure point of morals illustrates, he thinks, 'the vacuum that is created when a society no longer acknowledges a supreme spiritual authority'.[17] Of course no problem arises 'for one who takes the extreme view that society and the law have no concern at all with morals and that a man may behave as he wishes so long as he respects another's physical person and property'. But it is generally accepted that this is not enough, so the question has to be faced how morality is to be determined in the absence of a spiritual authority.

Lord Devlin takes his critics to be holding that it can be done 'by accepting the sovereignty of reason which will direct the conscience of every man to the same conclusion'.

But then the question arises: 'As men of reason are all men equal? If they are ... there can be no objection to morality being a matter for the popular vote. The objection is sustainable only upon the view that the opinion of the trained and educated mind, reached as its owner believes by an unimpassioned rational process, is as a source of morals superior to the opinion of ordinary men.'[18] But this claim is open to insuperable objections both practical and theoretical, practical, because moral philosophers notoriously disagree; theoretical, because 'what is obtained except to substitute for the voice of God the voice of the Superior Person?'

Up to this point Lord Devlin appears to be skilfully fastening upon his opponents the opprobrium of taking the educated man to be a superior source of morals to the man in the street or the man in the jury box. 'Make sure', his argument seems to run, 'that the ordinary man is adequately instructed, enabled to listen to the argument and given time to deliberate

[16] p. 91 [17] p. 92. [18] p. 93.

about it, and his opinion is as likely to be right as any other.'
If this is his view, it is easy to see that it does not exclude social
research and rational discussion upon the fullest possible
scale, but presupposes it. If this is his view Mr. Hughes would
be quite wrong in saying that 'the danger of Lord Devlin's
approach is that an established evaluation of collective judgements in society should replace the social research that is
necessary'.[19] But no sooner has one decided to interpret him in
this sense than Lord Devlin emphasizes once again that
whether ordinary people are right does not matter. 'I have said
that a sense of right and wrong is necessary for the life of a community. It is not necessary that their appreciation of right and
wrong, tested in the light of one set or another of those abstract
propositions about which men forever dispute, should be
correct. If it were, only one society at most could survive. What
the law-maker has to ascertain is not the true belief but the
common belief.'

So his critics, it seems, are right after all. What is morality,
for the purpose of the law, is to be determined by counting
heads, and inquiry into the reasonableness of the morality so
determined is superfluous. We are committed to the view that
the positive morality of a given society is beyond criticism.
Apartheid must be accepted in South Africa, genocide in Nazi
Germany. If the test is survival, any surviving society, however
unjust, has automatically passed the test.

But, mercifully, Lord Devlin is not consistent. For there
are a number of considerations which militate against this
interpretation. There is, first, his insistence on the 'reasonable'
or 'right-minded man'. He is evidently not to be identified
with the average man. Some *standard* is implied which many,
perhaps most, but not all men satisfy. There are, of course,
difficulties with this conception. 'Many critics,' Professor Hart
writes, 'might object that the "right minded person" cannot
be identified without circularity or that both he and the "reasonable man" whose views can be ascertained "without counting heads" are likely to be merely a projection of the judge's

[19] p. 675.

own morality or that of the social class to which he belongs.'[20]
A right-minded man, that is, can only be a man whom the
speaker for the time being regards as right-minded and his
judgement can only be based on the extent to which he shares
the speaker's moral attitudes. Hence to determine the common
morality by reference to the view of the right-minded man is in
the end to determine it by reference to one's own views. This
is the argument that has commonly been brought against
Aristotle's proposal to make the wise man the 'rule and
measure of virtue'. Like many philosophical arguments it is
too neat to be wholly convincing. If it were correct it would be
logically impossible to go to a wise man for advice, because
in judging him to be wise one would already have made for
oneself the moral decisions one hoped he would help one to
make. Yet this is something we all have experience of doing.
All the same, the objection does show that in deciding that
someone is right-minded we have to exercise *some* moral judgement. It is not simply a matter of empirical fact. (Whether we
call it a matter of fact at all depends on how generous we are
prepared to be in the use of the word 'fact'.) Moreover, agreement as to who is right-minded may well be less easy to secure
than Lord Devlin thinks. That this is so may be partly obscured
by the fact that the very expression 'right-minded' has a conservative, old-fashioned ring about it. People who use it do
probably agree very largely as to its application; but then those
whose moral outlook is different simply do not use the word.
They are more likely to talk about the 'enlightened man'. And
nothing is clearer than that 'enlightened men' and 'right-
minded men' tend to disagree on a wide range of issues. His
failure to notice this illustrates the tendency to which Professor
Hart calls attention in Lord Devlin's writings, to overestimate
the homogeneity of contemporary culture in this country. If
to accept someone as a right-minded or reasonable man involves some moral judgement, Lord Devlin cannot be wholly
indifferent to the 'correctness' of the common morality. He

[20] *The Morality of the Criminal Law*, p. 41.

has to *judge* that the ordinary man is likely to be as good a source of morals as the sophisticated intellectual.

But is he aware of this implication? It appears not, for he constantly returns to the theme that the *quality* of the morality does not matter. Is there, then, perhaps, after all a morally neutral way of identifying right-minded men? Two possibilities might be suggested. Right-minded people may be people who, for whatever reason, are especially characteristic of a society, or influential in it, whose attitudes are, in fact, the dominant ones. If what matters about morality, from the standpoint of society is, as Lord Devlin insists, its cohesive character, the morality which has the best chance of continuing to maintain cohesion, it might be said, is that of the most settled, stable, and influential groups, people who 'have a stake in the country'. This is, perhaps, the conception underlying the old rule that jurymen should be householders. Alternatively, if, as Professor Hart, and many other moral philosophers from Plato onwards, have maintained, there are principles of conduct which must be recognized and, to some minimum degree, observed, in any stable society, it should be possible to identify them and to recommend them simply upon this pragmatic ground. People who habitually observe these principles, in no matter what society, must be contributing powerfully to its cohesion. They are 'right-minded men' and it could be argued that their contribution to the stability of society would be reinforced by the operation of any other principles of conduct, which all or most of them happen to share.

Along such lines as these it might be possible to discover a justification for the enforcement of morals which took no account of the 'correctness' of the morality enforced. Perhaps something of the sort is what Lord Devlin intends. But if one takes the whole range of his writings it is hard to believe that it is. For he is prepared, in speaking of the role of intellectuals in law reform, to talk about change from the law as it is to the law as it ought to be, and, in criticizing Mill, he insists that rulers must be free to act upon what they believe. 'What we believe to be evil may indeed be evil and we cannot forever condemn ourselves to inactivity against evil because of the chance that we may by mistake destroy good. *For better or for worse the law-maker must act according to his lights'* [21] [my italics]. No doubt, given sufficient ingenuity, these references to 'good' and 'evil', 'ought' and 'ought not' *could* be construed in the sense required by Lord Devlin's official theory, i.e. in terms of a society's positive morality actual or potential, but it would be a forced interpretation out of keeping with Lord Devlin's intense moral seriousness in these passages. Consider the final paragraph of the chapter on 'Democracy and Morality':

To hold that morality is a question of fact is not to deify the *status quo* or to deny the perfectibility of man. The unending search for truth goes on and so does the struggle towards the perfect society. It is our common creed that no society can be perfect unless it is a free society.... In the free society there are men, fighters for freedom, who strain at the bonds of their society, having a vision of life as they feel it ought to be.... What they gain and as they gain it becomes the property of their society and is to be kept. The law is its keeper. So there are others, defenders and not attackers, but also fighting for freedom, for those who defend a free society defend freedom. These others are those who serve the law. They do not look up too often to the heights of what ought to be, lest they lose sight of the ground on which they stand and which it is their duty to defend— the law as it is, morality as it is, freedom as it is—none of them perfect but the things that their society has got and must not let go.[22]

There are, in fact, conservatives and radicals. The radicals want the law to move from what it is to what it ought to be; the conservatives are anxious not to lose the good that has already been won. But neither is indifferent to the rational acceptability of the standards embodied in the law. This seems to be the clear implication of this passage.

How then is this position to be reconciled with the repeated insistence on the need for cohesion and the consequent concern with the *de facto* positive morality of an existing society?

It is worth noticing, before trying to answer this, that there

[21] p. 123.　　　　　[22] p. 100.

appears to be no necessary connexion between the claim that the law may be used to enforce morality and moral conservatism. It is true in our society that it is usually moral conservatives who want to enforce morality, but this could be because the morality which our existing law tends to enforce is a traditional, largely Christian morality, which many radicals regard as obsolescent. It is conceivable, however, that circumstances might arise in which radicals were in favour of enforcing an 'enlightened' morality. It is naturally not easy to find examples, but one is, perhaps, the Race Relations Act (bill presented in Parliament on 7 April 1965; Royal assent 8 November 1965). The controversial issue here was the proposal to substitute an intention to stir up hatred for an intention to stir up disorder and it was opposed from the Conservative benches precisely on the ground that it represented an attempt to invoke the law on a purely moral issue. *The Times* commented on 8 April that '... judging the criminality of utterances by reference to their subject matter and content rather than by reference to their likely effect upon public order ... the clause is in short an instrument of potential censorship'.

But from the government benches it was argued that '... it is far better to put this bill on the Statute Book now, before social stresses and ill-will have the chance of corrupting and distorting our relationships'.[23] Mr. David Ennals was even more forthright. He noted the opposition's concern for '... the freedom to stir up hatred against other groups'. He went on, 'I should not have thought that this was the sort of freedom that we would wish to preserve in our society.'[24] And later he said, 'I said earlier that the main object is to change the course of events, to change human behaviour. Sometimes, one cannot change human behaviour except by having the authority to punish.'[25]

It is, of course, true that incitement to racial hatred is likely, in the end, to result in acts of public disorder and this argument was also used in the debate. 'When hatred has been stored up, unfortunately history shows only too clearly that violence

---

[23] *Hansard*, vol. 711, p. 942.　　[24] p. 988.　　[25] p. 993.

and disorder are probably not far away.' To this extent the legislation could be justified on Professor Hart's criterion of preventing harm to others. But what is significant is the degree to which men of radical sympathies were prepared to back legislation with the clear and primary intention of improving the ethos of our society and protecting it from corruption by racialist propaganda. Here is an issue upon which radicals (rightly) have strong feelings as they generally do not about, e.g., obscenity, in relation to which, therefore, they employ very much the same language of reprobation as conservatives do about the dangers of pornography.

Lord Devlin's case for the enforcement of morals appears at first sight to be essentially bound up with moral conservatism. This is because he is primarily concerned with maintaining the cohesion of society and it is the existing morality which is doing that job. But, as we have seen, he is quite prepared to envisage a change in public morality and, although in his view the law should be slow to follow suit, it should do so eventually —as soon, that is, as the new morality is likely to prove more cohesive than the old. His attitude to a moral revolution is, in fact, analogous to the British government's attitude to a political revolution in a foreign country. It will be slow to recognize the new régime, but will generally do so as soon as it is satisfied that it has become the *de facto* government of the country. Does this mean that British governments are indifferent to the political complexion of foreign governments? Clearly not: where political influence can still affect the outcome, the British government will exercise it in favour of liberal democracy, but for diplomatic purposes it attaches much greater importance to effective power than to ideological acceptability.

Similarly, Lord Devlin need not be indifferent to the character of the morality that is to be enforced. It is open to him and to others who have strong and clearly articulated views to use their powers of persuasion in such a way as to influence the public debate. He points out that intellectuals are peculiarly well placed to do this. 'The popular vote does not itself enact or veto; rather, the initiative is put into the hands of a very few men. Under this method the law reformer has a double opportunity. He may work upon the popular opinion which is the law-maker's base or he may influence the law-maker directly. At each of these stages the educated man is at an advantage in a democratic society.'[26]

Not only is this in fact the case, but Lord Devlin clearly thinks it ought to be. Consider what he says about the second advantage. 'The other advantage which the educated man possesses is that he has easier access to the ear of the law-maker. I do not mean merely by lobbying. When—with such latitude as our democratic and judicial system allows—the law-maker is determining the pace and direction of his advance from the law that is towards the law that ought to be, *he does and should* inform himself of the views of wise and experienced men and pay extra attention to them'[27] (my italics). And he goes on to enumerate cases in which a minority has had success in the reform of the criminal law recently in England.

'But,' it may be asked, 'is this consistent with Lord Devlin's conception of the task of the legislator as that of determining and declaring the existing common morality?' *Ought* the legislator, on this view, to pay particular attention to the views of 'wise and experienced men' or of 'ardent minorities'? Well, as we have seen, the common morality, for Lord Devlin's purposes, is not just the morality of the majority or of the average man; it is the morality of the reasonable or right-minded man: it is the morality of the most stable and influential sections of society, and it might be argued that educated opinion should have special weight as possessing these qualifications to an eminent degree.

Would Lord Devlin's critics be mollified by an interpretation of his position along these lines? If not, at what point would they part company from him?

The argument concerns Lord Devlin's proposals for *ascertaining* the morality which should be enforced. Some of his critics do not want *any* morality enforced, so that the question

[26] p. 95.   [27] p. 96.

'Which morality?' is not one which they themselves would see any need to answer. They believe the law should concern itself solely with the prevention of harm and they want the content of the law to be determined so far as possible by a rational consideration, backed by the fullest available research, of the most effective ways of combating the evils to be prevented. It follows, however, on the hypothesis that the law may be used to enforce morality, that the morality to be enforced should be a rational morality, capable of withstanding critical scrutiny. But if this is so, it will not be enough, as Lord Devlin suggests, to 'pay extra attention' to wise and experienced men. The *sole* considerations that should be before the mind of the legislators are rational ones backed, wherever possible, by scientific evidence.

Is then no attention to be paid to the opinions of the ordinary man? Is the state of public opinion irrelevant to the question what the content of the law should be? Surely not, for the law will be ineffective if it is too far ahead of (or behind) public opinion. For pragmatic reasons the law and common morality must not be too much out of step, and, on grounds of general democratic principle, popular opinion must be treated with respect.

There has lain undetected in the background of this discussion what Professor Wollheim has called 'the paradox of democracy'.[28] The citizen believes that the best policy ought to be enacted; but, as a democrat, he also believes that whatever policy emerges from the democratic process ought to be enacted. The two need not, and often will not, coincide. The democrat's duty is to do his best to influence the democratic process in such a way that the policy he believes to be right is accepted and to co-operate loyally with whatever policy is finally adopted. This latter is not an overriding obligation, since the right to rebel against even a democratic government pursuing unjust policies cannot be denied. All the parties to this debate are believers in a free society and can be presumed

[28] See: 'A Paradox in the Theory of Democracy', in *Philosophy, Politics and Society* (second series), ed. Laslett and Runciman, pp 71 ff.

to agree to these propositions. Hence when Mr. Hughes pleads for rational legislation based on adequate social research, he is not denying the right of the ordinary man to have the last word. When Lord Devlin wants the law to listen to 'the man in the Clapham omnibus', he is, in part at least, simply pleading for democratic processes. It may be that both parties have not borne clearly in mind the distinction between the two questions: (i) What considerations should determine legislation? Answer: rational moral and political arguments, backed up, wherever possible, by adequate social research, and (ii) How should the final decision be made, when opinions differ? Answer: by democratic procedures, i.e. in accordance with the wishes of the people, *ordinary* people like the man in the Clapham omnibus. It looks sometimes as if Lord Devlin is offering as his answer to the first question the answer that should be given to the second; i.e. he is saying that legislation should be based on the moral opinions of the common man and he is accusing his opponents of being undemocratic for not agreeing with him. And *they* sometimes seem to be offering in reply to the second question an answer appropriate only to the first, i.e. that the final decision should be that of trained sociologists. To the extent that they think this they are, indeed, undemocratic.

Nevertheless I think we must conclude that Lord Devlin is not *merely* pleading for democratic processes. He does want, by legislation, to enforce the morality of the man in the Clapham omnibus (not all, but some of it), *because it serves to promote the cohesion of society*. But even on this point I am inclined to think that Lord Devlin and his opponents differ in emphasis only (though they differ *considerably* in emphasis). Lord Devlin attaches primary importance to the cohesive effect of the shared institutions and common morality of a society. Rather than risk weakening that he would forego or postpone reforms which are on general grounds desirable. But he is not opposed to all change and, when change comes, he wants it to be in the right direction and he wants full use to be made of any methods which will help to determine what is the right direction (though he appears to be less sanguine than his opponents about the possibility of getting agreement about them). His critics reverse the priorities. What matters most to them is to get the right answer or, at any rate, the reasonable answer. But they also recognize the importance of public feeling for the effectiveness of the law, so that it must be, where possible, educated and always taken into account.

A possible analogy is provided by school uniform. (Compare the recent discussions at Eton upon this subject.) Suppose it to be agreed that one of the justifications for having a school uniform is that it strengthens the children's sense of belonging to an institution to which they owe a certain loyalty. Nevertheless a uniform is a set of clothes and clothes can be judged by 'rational' standards of suitability, comfort, appearance, and hygiene. Lord Devlin wants to maintain the existing, old-fashioned, possibly unhygienic uniform for as long as the children are content to wear it. It provides cohesion. It will not be easy to get people to agree on a more sensible, healthy uniform and it will in any case take time. So stick to the old uniform, he says, until some definite alternative wins general acceptance. Above all avoid, if you possibly can, a state of affairs in which most of the children have become discontented with the old uniform without yet being prepared to accept any other, for this threatens the whole point of having a uniform.

His critics are rationalists. What matters most to them is that the children should wear sensible clothes, and this is something for which rational, even scientific, criteria are available. So, they say, get a new uniform designed as quickly as possible. Of course, the children must be willing to wear it or it won't perform its function; they must be educated to it and, so long as they object, the reform must be postponed as being impracticable. But this is the only weight to be given to the children's attachment to the existing uniform.

We could work in the 'paradox of democracy' by supposing that Eton decides these matters by popular vote—but perhaps that would strain the parable overmuch.

4

The Law's Concern with Morality: Why is Bigamy Illegal?

Up to this point I have discussed Professor Hart's positive views primarily in their bearing upon Lord Devlin's thesis. I want now to consider them in their own right.

Professor Hart takes his stand with the Wolfenden Committee upon the famous principle in Mill's *Essay on Liberty*.[1]

That principle is, that the sole end for which mankind are warranted, individually or collectively, in interfering with the liberty of action of any of their number, is self-protection. That the only purpose for which power can be rightfully exercised over any member of a civilized community, against his will, is to prevent harm to others. His own good, either physical or moral, is not a sufficient warrant. He cannot rightfully be compelled to do or forbear because it will be better for him to do so, because it will make him happier, because, in the opinion of others, to do so would be wise, or even right.

He does, however, wish to amend the principle in one important respect to allow a place for 'paternalism—the protection of people against themselves'. 'Mill,' he says, 'no doubt might have protested against a paternalistic policy of using the law to protect even a consenting victim from bodily harm nearly as much as he protested against laws used merely to enforce positive morality; but this does not mean that these two policies are identical.'[2]

It is too often assumed [he continues later[3]] that if a law is not designed to protect one man from another its only rationale can be

---

[1] p. 73.   [2] *Law, Liberty and Morality*, p. 31.   [3] p. 34.

that it is designed to punish moral wickedness or, in Lord Devlin's words, 'to enforce a moral principle'. Thus it is often urged that statutes punishing cruelty to animals can only be explained in that way. But it is certainly intelligible, both as an account of the original motives inspiring such legislation and as the specification of an aim widely held to be worth pursuing, to say that the law is here concerned with the *suffering*, albeit only of animals, rather than with the immorality of torturing them. Certainly no one who supports this use of the criminal law is thereby bound in consistency to admit that the law may punish forms of immorality which involve no suffering to any sentient being.

The principle, as amended, is that the law may be used only to prevent harm to the individual himself or to others. Professor Hart notes[4] that the principle has been criticized on two different, and indeed inconsistent, grounds. The first is that '"No man is an island"; and in an organised society it is impossible to identify classes of actions which harm no one or no one but the individual who does them.' The second is that, although such a division may be made, 'it is merely dogmatic on Mill's part to limit legal coercion to the class of actions which harm others'.

Oddly enough, while Professor Hart devotes a great deal of attention to the second of these arguments, he says very little about the first. This may be because he chooses to concentrate mainly on sexual morality 'where it seems *prima facie* plausible that there are actions immoral by accepted standards and yet not harmful to others'.[5] Even here, however, he might, perhaps, have been expected to inquire whether this *prima facie* plausibility would stand examination.

The first thing we are likely to notice, if we examine it, is that the concept of 'harm' is both vague and controversial. If 'harm' is restricted to physical injury or deterioration the claim is, indeed, plausible that sexual deviations commonly considered immoral do not cause harm. But if the law is invoked, as it is by the Wolfenden Committee, to prevent public indecency, the concept of 'harm' must at least be stretched to cover offence as well as injury. For the Wolfenden Committee seek 'to protect the citizens from what is offensive or injurious'. As soon as offence is admitted to be harmful the way is open, as Professor Hart recognizes, to an almost unlimited extension, 'for offence is given also when those who condemn certain sexual practices as immoral learn that others indulge them in private'.[6] Professor Hart suggests two ways of meeting this argument. It might be claimed (a) that such distress is not 'harm', (b) that it is 'harm' but so slight as to be outweighed by the misery occasioned by punishment. But, he says, 'the fundamental objection surely is that the right to be protected from the distress which is inseparable from the bare knowledge that others are acting in ways you think are wrong cannot be acknowledged by anyone who recognizes individual liberty as a value.'[7] In this he is, of course, right, but it is to be noticed that what he is appealing to here is the overriding importance of a countervailing value—individual liberty, and not just the principle that only acts which harm others are to be prohibited. If *this* principle alone is to be appealed to, the only way out is (a), to deny that such distress constitutes harm.

But, if this principle is to do the job the Wolfenden Committee require it to do, the concept of 'harm' must be stretched still further. For they wish to use the law to 'provide sufficient safeguards against exploitation and corruption of others, particularly those who are specially vulnerable, because they are young, weak in body or mind, inexperienced or in a state of special physical, official or economic dependence'. On any ordinary understanding of the word, to protect people from 'corruption' is to protect them from moral harm. Lord Devlin pushes home this point in his essay on 'Morals and Contemporary Social Reality'.[8] The question is, what is the scope of paternalism? Professor Hart has modified Mill's thesis to accommodate a degree of paternalism. 'But will that be complete paternalism, i.e., in respect of all that makes a man better and happier? Or is a distinction being drawn between a man's physical good and his moral good? Is Professor Hart, so to speak, a physical paternalist and a moral individualist?'[9]

[6] p. 45.   [7] p. 46.   [8] *The Enforcement of Morals*, ch. VII.   [9] p. 133.

The dilemma in which Professor Hart appears to be placed is this. Does he wish to limit paternalism to the prevention of physical harm (in which we may include, although Lord Devlin does not mention it, offence)? In that case the law has no right to protect anyone from 'corruption'. Or does he wish to extend paternalism so as to include protection from moral harm? In that case (*a*) he will, if he is to rescue his original thesis, need to draw a distinction between moral paternalism and the enforcement of morality—the one permissible, the other not—(*b*) he will have to concede, in any case, that there is no realm of private morality and immorality that is not the law's business.

Professor Hart has not yet indicated how he would deal with this dilemma, but the challenge has to some extent been taken up by Mr. Hughes.[10] He does so in reply to a passage in Lord Devlin's Maccabaean Lecture: 'If society is not prepared to say that homosexuality is morally wrong, there would be no basis for a law protecting youth from "corruption" or punishing a man for living on the "immoral earnings" of a homosexual prostitute, as the Wolfenden Report recommends.'[11] Lord Devlin is maintaining that the principle recognized by the law in these cases is that of 'moral paternalism' (in the terminology of his later essay). In reply to this Mr. Hughes observes that 'the drinking of alcohol is not generally regarded as immoral in itself, yet there are laws prohibiting minors from drinking on licensed premises. Heterosexual activity is not *per se* immoral, yet there are laws prohibiting assaults on young girls (even with their consent) and laws making it criminal to live on the earnings of a female prostitute. To prohibit acts of a similar nature in a homosexual context need not involve a general judgement about homosexual acts between consenting adults.'[12]

It would appear that in the case of penalties for living upon the 'immoral' earnings of female prostitutes a moral judgement is clearly implied; but this case could be dealt with simply by denying that the law ought, in fact, to concern itself

---

[10] p. 673.   [11] p. 8.   [12] p. 674.

E

with it. It would be harder to maintain that the law should not concern itself with the corruption of minors, which is, accordingly, a more stubborn example.

It is of course true that there are things which we regard as bad for children, though entirely permissible for adults. So we cannot presume, from the mere fact that the law does not allow children to do or suffer something that it regards it as immoral when done or suffered by adults. But in order to refute Lord Devlin, it is not enough to point this out. It is necessary to show (a) that the law's interference in the case of children is not prompted by a concern for their moral welfare, (b) that in cases where such concern is admitted it does not presuppose any judgement as to the morality of the relevant behaviour among adults. And it is, surely, difficult to show either of these things. It is reasonable to suppose that the rule against allowing children in bars is intended not only to prevent them getting drunk now, but also to prevent them growing up with a tendency to drunkenness. Similarly with sexual assaults. We may contrast, in this case, the legislation prohibiting sexual intercourse with a girl under sixteen with the law prohibiting marriage under that age. The latter law embodies a judgement that what is suitable for an adult is not suitable for a child; the former law, it is reasonable to suppose, also manifests a concern that the girl should not be 'corrupted', i.e. should not become habituated to a pattern of conduct which is commonly held to be immoral when practised among adults (though it is not then prohibited by the criminal law).

It can scarcely be denied that the use of the word 'corruption' indicates pretty clearly the law's present concern with morality in these cases. But it might, nevertheless, be argued that, even though, historically speaking, moral concern has guided the development of these laws, they *can* be justified on non-moral grounds and should be maintained only in so far as they can be so justified. Thus it might be maintained that, in a society which, for whatever reasons, condemns certain behaviour as immoral it ought to be a punishable offence to induce the young to adopt a form of life which, given the prevailing intolerance, is likely to make them unhappy. An adult should be free to make an 'experiment in living' which may involve persecution, but a child ought not to be committed to such a course, which would normally be against the will of its parents. This argument would give considerable weight, albeit indirectly, to the *de facto* positive morality of a particular society; and in such a fashion that moral criticism of that morality would be irrelevant. All that matters is that public attitudes are strong enough to be likely to produce unhappiness. In a society that was strongly anti-Semitic it would seem to justify making it a criminal offence to habituate children to the company of Jews, even though the morality involved is open to serious criticism. There may sometimes be a place for this sort of paternalism, but as an agent of conformity it would appear more dangerous than straightforward moral paternalism, for the latter requires the moral case to be explicitly argued.

A different criterion which might be appealed to is that of 'psychological harm'. Children, it could be argued, suffer psychological harm, if they are introduced to sexual experience prematurely and this is the justification for the sort of legislation we are considering. Thus, if 'physical paternalism' is supplemented by 'psychological paternalism' it can do all the work required without our having to invoke 'moral paternalism'. It has also, it might be claimed, the great advantage of basing the law upon a criterion that is susceptible of scientific research.

This appears to be the criterion favoured by Dr. Alex Comfort in his book, *Sex in Society*. Writing about obscenity he says,

The conventional assertion—indeed, the legal definition, under both the Cockburn Rule and the Obscene Publications Act—is that pornography can or does 'corrupt'. If this means that it does *tangible psychological harm* (my italics), the assertion might be true if it specified what matter is harmful and to whom, but we have no means of knowing this, for no study has ever been published to demonstrate the ill-effects of such matter, as the ill-effects of guilt-centred hygiene literature have been demonstrated, or those of violence in comic-books inferred.[13]

This criterion of 'tangible psychological harm' is recommended as being susceptible of scientific test. It is presupposed that we have access to a value-free concept of mental health. That this is so is, indeed, widely believed. 'In the United States', says Lady Wootton, ' "the women's magazines and other mass media" it is said, "are telling how to 'get' mental health and how not to 'lose' it as if it were as tangible as a permanent wave." '[14] Unfortunately, as Lady Wootton argues in this invigorating chapter on 'Social Pathology and the Concept of Mental Health', 'Long indeed is the road to be travelled before we can hope to reach a definition of mental-cum-physical health, which is objective, scientific and wholly free of social value-judgements.'[15]

The principal difficulty arises from the tendency to define mental health in terms of social adjustment, so that the aim of therapy should be to adjust the individual to the demands of his society. Thus:

Moloney describes how the authoritarian mores of the Japanese conflict with the psychoanalytic aim of creating free, adaptable individuals. The aim of therapy in psychiatric (as distinct from psychoanalytic) practice should, he thinks, be frankly to adjust the patient to the demands of his society; but for the psychoanalyst, the answer to the question 'to be or not to be free?' he finds more difficult. 'Should the American and the Japanese psychoanalytic therapist', he asks, 'encourage individualism or should they insist upon insensible and unconscious submissive conformity to the existing culture?' ... 'The Japanese psychoanalyst, faced with the problem of curing a mentally ill person, must first of all diagnose him as "ill" because he does not adhere to the rigidly prescribed culture patterns I have outlined. The "cure" upon which the analyst then embarks constitutes the opposite of a cure by western standards. Instead of endeavouring, as do occidental psychoanalysts, to free the individual from his inner thongs, the Japanese analyst actually tightens those thongs.'[16]

The problem is inescapable so long as mental health is

[13] p. 76.   [14] *Social Science and Social Pathology*, p. 210.
[15] p. 225.   [16] p. 218.

defined in terms of adjustment to the demands of society, and, so long as this is so, as Lady Wootton puts it, 'Value-soaked definitions and explanations ... leave the scientific, objective status of the concept of mental health in a decidedly shaky condition.'[17]

The alternative proposal fares no better—to define mental health in terms of adjustment, not to an existing society, but to an ideal society, does no more than substitute explicit for implicit value-judgements. And there seems no prospect of defining it without any reference to anti-social behaviour.

Dr. Comfort's own discussion betrays clear evidence of his own ethical position. Thus he evidently believes that to feel guilt about any aspect of sexual behaviour is psychologically unhealthy. 'The objective of sexual studies today is therefore fairly clear-cut—to determine, on a basis of factual research, the types of conduct best suited to the realization of mental and physical health, and ... by a cooperative effort with education and psychiatry to end the long-standing association between sexuality and guilt.'[18] It looks as if the mere presence of guilt associated with some forms of sexual behaviour will be regarded by Dr. Comfort as, at least, *prima facie* evidence of psychological harm. This presupposes the moral judgement that there is no sexual behaviour that one ought to feel guilty about. His position is, admittedly, somewhat extreme. A more plausible approach would be to distinguish between normal and pathological guilt and most psychiatrists would, in fact, discriminate in this way. But 'normal guilt' implies reference to a norm, to some standard of appropriateness; and the question 'What sort of behaviour is it appropriate to feel guilty about?' is not one which can be answered independently of moral judgement. But suppose we were satisfied that a sexual assault on a child had done the child no physical or psychological harm, however defined, or even that such acts, considered as a class, had no tendency to do so, should we be content that the law should disinterest itself in such conduct?

It seems to me that we very well might not. If so, what would

[17] p. 220.   [18] p. 83.

be the nature of our concern? It is natural to say that it would be for the moral welfare of the children, since they might be led to form a wrong conception of the nature and purpose of sexual activity. Of course, our conception of this is very much conditioned by our culture, and other cultures could be found without difficulty which have no objection to patterns of conduct which we prohibit, and even encourage them. The special concern which the law shows for the immature and which the Wolfenden Report shows no desire to lessen is based, presumably, upon the conviction that children should be protected from influences likely to prevent them becoming good and acceptable members of society, where what is good and acceptable reflects the basic ideals of our society. For this reason the law cannot remain and does not remain wholly neutral as to what *are* the basic ideals of our society.

No doubt many of the children so protected will grow up to be rather imperfect representatives of these ideals and some of them will wish to repudiate them altogether. If enough of them do so, the ideals will change. But education involves handing on a traditional way of life as well as developing a capacity for criticism. Hence if sexual behaviour is considered an important aspect of our total way of life, as it inevitably is, the young must be given some indication what the sexual ideal is. This belongs to education and, perhaps, to informal rather than formal education, but the State has a legitimate concern with influences which might strikingly interfere with the educational process. Hence it is prepared to intervene in order to protect, e.g. those who are in 'moral danger'.

The law's concern with 'corruption' is, it would seem, a clear case of its concern with morality. There are, however, a number of cases where the basis of legal intervention is not so clear. One of these is indecency. We have seen that Professor Hart justifies the law of bigamy as an attempt to protect religious feelings from offence by a public act desecrating the ceremony.[19] He takes the example of bigamy to show 'the need to distinguish between the immorality of a practice and its

[19] *Law, Liberty and Morality*, p. 41.

aspect as a public offensive act or nuisance'. Bigamy is not, as we have seen, a very good example of the distinction, but the distinction is an important one nevertheless. Professor Hart points out that the Romans distinguished the province of the Censor, concerned with morals, from that of the Aedile concerned with public decency. He complains of Lord Simonds's indifference to this distinction in Shaw's case: 'It matters little what label is given to the offending act. To one of your Lordships it may appear an affront to public decency, to another considering that it may succeed in its obvious intention of provoking libidinous desires it will seem a corruption of public morals.'[20]

Yet, as Professor Hart points out, 'sexual intercourse between husband and wife is not immoral, but if it takes place in public it is an affront to public decency. Homosexual intercourse between consenting adults in private is immoral according to conventional morality, but not an affront to public decency, though it would be both if it took place in public.'[21] He adds that, 'The recent English law relating to prostitution attends to this difference. It has not made prostitution a crime, but punishes its public manifestation in order to protect the ordinary citizen, who is an unwilling witness of it in the streets, from something offensive.'

Here Professor Hart shows conclusively that indecency is to be distinguished from immorality and that the law often punishes conduct as indecent and not as immoral. Hence in accepting existing legislation against indecency he is not committed to approving legislation against immorality.

It is necessary at this point to recur to a distinction which was introduced earlier between two possible positions which Lord Devlin's opponents may wish to occupy. They may wish to maintain, as Professor Hart clearly does, that the criminal law should not be used to enforce morality. They may also wish to maintain that the law, whether criminal or civil, should not concern itself with questions of morality at all further than is necessary to its purpose of protecting individuals from 'tan-

[20] (1961) 2 A.E.R. at 452, quoted by Hart, p. 44.   [21] p. 45.

gible' harm. In particular the law should not presuppose any judgements about sexual morality, which, on this view, are properly matters for personal decision.

This distinction is relevant to the question of indecency. For it is not clear that in its attitude to indecency the law is morally neutral. This can be seen if we ask why certain actions cause offence. Consider the presence of prostitutes upon the streets. The mere fact that people are being accosted is not enough to give offence. One is not 'offended' by a pavement artist seeking alms or by a child demanding a penny for the guy. The offence is associated with the knowledge that the soliciting is being done with a view to prostitution and it would not be objected to, or would be objected to very much less, if prostitution were regarded as morally acceptable. An innocent who had no idea what these women were doing would not be offended. Even in the case of sexual intercourse being performed in public there is, perhaps, an element of moral judgement. As Lord Devlin argues, 'If we thought that un-restricted indulgence in the sexual passions was as good a way of life as any other for those who liked it, we should find nothing indecent in the practice of it either in public or in private. It would become no more indecent than kissing in public. Decency as an objective depends on the belief in con-tinence as a virtue which requires sexual activity to be kept within prescribed bounds.'[22] This goes too far, for we also regard as indecent the exercise of excretory functions in public and here there is no question of moral condemnation. But it is difficult not to believe that our attitude to sexual intercourse in public owes something to our conviction that this is a matter which should be subject to strict *moral* control. This is one of a number of cases where it is reasonable to suppose that the law is guided by a variety of considerations. The prevention of offence is certainly the principal one, but it is not wholly in-dependent of the moral assessment of the offending acts.

Another case is that of cruelty to animals. Lord Devlin seems to regard this as a clear instance of legislation designed to

[22] p. 120.

enforce morality.[23] Professor Hart replies sensibly enough, that the law's concern might well be with 'the suffering, albeit only of animals, rather than with the immorality of torturing them'. It is possible, however, that both are right. It is certainly an object of policy to prevent suffering to animals,[24] but does this exhaust our interest in the matter? May we not also be concerned to prevent the degradation that goes with cruelty to animals? Is it plausible to maintain that the prohibition in this country of bull-fighting and cock-fighting reflects solely our concern for the suffering of bulls and cocks? We permit experiments on animals which may involve suffering (though this is kept to a minimum) on the ground that they contribute to the advancement of knowledge and the control of disease in human beings, these being regarded as legitimate human interests which outweigh the interest of the animals themselves. The enjoyment which many people might derive from bull-fighting or cock-fighting is not allowed to count in this way. Why not? In part, surely, because we view with moral condemnation enjoyment derived from the infliction of pain upon sentient creatures; it is not a legitimate interest which we are prepared to recognize. Normally, of course, this consideration only enters in when pain is in fact inflicted, so that it tends to be masked by the simple desire to prevent pain. In order to isolate it, we should have to suppose a situation in which pain was believed to be inflicted, but was not, such as a bull-fight in which the bull was anaesthetized, although its sensory and motor responses remained unaffected.

The example is too unreal to be serviceable, but we might consider instead two different cases. One is that of commercialized all-in wrestling. Here there is a good deal of apparent brutality, which is said to be largely feigned (I have no means of knowing whether it is). Sheer enjoyment in the infliction of pain is part of its appeal and it is accordingly condemned by many as 'degrading'. It differs from cruelty to animals in that the wrestlers have consented to it and are, apparently, happy to earn their living in this way. A move to get it prohibited by

[23] p. 17.   [24] The point is well made by Mr. Hughes, p. 676.

law would have to rely on (*a*) its offensiveness, (*b*) its degradation, the former not being wholly independent of the latter; it
is offensive, in part, *because* degrading. Defenders of all-in
wrestling would argue that the spectators enjoy it and that
what they enjoy is not the sheer infliction of pain for its own
sake, but a good, clean fight—or if not a clean fight, at least a
fair fight in the sense of one to which both parties have consented. To enjoy a scrap is not reprehensible, as it would be to
enjoy the infliction of pain for its own sake. The other example
is that of the 'theatre of cruelty', for here too the audience,
caught up in the dramatic illusion, 'believes' that pain is being
inflicted, though in fact it is not. Yet questions of censorship
notoriously arise with regard to such performances. Why? The
prima facie case for censorship cannot rest on the fact that pain
is being inflicted on those portrayed as suffering. In part it
rests on the belief that those who watch such representations
are liable themselves to be prompted to acts of cruelty. In part
it rests, undoubtedly, on the principle of preventing offence
to the audience. The experience for the audience in watching
such simulated violence is painful in the sense of 'shocking'.
Some dislike the representation of violence as such; others are
morally outraged by unjustified and insensate violence. Others,
however, may enjoy it; but to pander to such perverted appe-
tites may be condemned as 'degrading'.

The case against censorship is twofold; on the one hand there
are general arguments against any kind of censorship, as an
unwarranted interference with liberty. On the other there are
particular arguments against censorship of the representations
of violence. Violence is a fact of our world; we must learn to
face it. The dramatist's aim is not to commend, but to condemn
violence; he cannot convey his message if his palette is robbed
of its darker colours. These latter arguments presuppose that
there *is* a case for censorship where appeal is being made to no
other motive than the love of cruelty. To intervene in such a
case would not be to interfere 'unwarrantably'.

The issues were revealed in an illuminating way in a tele-
vision interview with Peter Hall, in which he was questioned

about 'the theatre of cruelty'.[25] James Mossman asked him (apropos of censorship):

Assuming that young people, to use that slightly self-conscious expression, are not as sensitive or as shockable as the present Lord Chamberlain, what is the limit beyond which you could corrupt or degrade by a book, a play, or a film?

Mr. Hall replied,

You can degrade, surely, by literal obscenity on the stage. But then it would not be art, or theatre ... Art—the image, not the fact—cannot degrade and corrupt, though it certainly upsets and disturbs ...

Here, as Bernard Levin subsequently pointed out in the discussion, Peter Hall is defining 'art' to suit his thesis. More precisely he is so defining 'art' that 'art cannot corrupt or degrade' becomes a tautology. As an argument against theatrical censorship as such it fails because it assumes that theatrical performances which had a tendency to degrade or corrupt could properly be censored—though they would not, of course, be 'art'.

All-in wrestling is not prohibited by law. Theatrical censorship can, and no doubt does, prohibit certain representations of violence. The point is that the case for or against legal intervention relies in part upon such moral considerations as the effect upon the character of the spectators and the inherent degradation of the spectacle, so that it becomes a relevant issue whether the violence exhibited or portrayed is or is not designed simply to appeal to the motive of cruelty. The examples were chosen so as to eliminate, as far as possible, the complicating factor of the actual suffering inflicted. However, if the law has some concern in *these* cases with the moral effect of the performances, the same concern may well be present in legislation against cruelty to animals in addition to the primary concern with the suffering of the animals themselves.

I have chosen to discuss cruelty to animals and other manifestations of cruelty because the wrongness of cruelty is universally accepted. No one would wish to deny that cruelty was degrading or that someone who had become habituated to it

²⁵ *Listener*, 19 November 1964, vol. 72, p. 790.

had thereby been corrupted. About obscenity, in the ordinary sense of the word, there is less agreement. Yet the law does seek to control it under the Obscene Publications Act 1959. Evidence may be given, as it was on a massive scale in the 'Lady Chatterley' trial, to show 'that publication of the article in question is justified as being for the public good on the ground that it is in the interests of science, literature, art or learning, or of other objects of general concern'. The issue of obscenity remains in the hands of the jury, who have to decide whether the merits of the publication are so high as to outbalance the obscenity. The Act seeks, in effect, to strike a balance between the interests of free speech and those of morality. That obscenity is thought of in moral terms is evident from the statutory definition. The test is 'whether the tendency of the matter charged as obscenity is to deprave and corrupt those whose minds are open to such immoral influences and into whose hands a publication of this sort may fall'.[26]

There are a number of notorious puzzles in connexion with 'the tendency to deprave and corrupt'. Can a person be corrupted more than once? The Courts have held that he can. Can a policeman be corrupted, he being *ex hypothesi* incorruptible? 'In *Clayton and Halsey*, for example, two experienced policemen—who must, in the words of an appeal judge, have been clad in a "spiritual asbestos"—were obliged to argue in cross-examination that the allegedly obscene articles which they had purchased aroused no feelings at all; and the Court of Criminal Appeal had no option but to quash the convictions...'[27] These problems are largely avoided by the American courts, which define obscene material as 'material which deals with sex in a manner appealing to prurient interest'. On this Mr. Williams comments,

Though it can be argued that sexual thoughts and desires can be aroused in very many ways apart from by obscenity, the orthodox view at the present time is expressed by an American judge: that the legislature 'can reasonably draw the inference that over a long

[26] See D. G. T. Williams, 'Sex and Morals 1954-63' in *The Criminal Law Review*, April 1964.
[27] Williams, *op. cit.*, p. 262.

period of time the indiscriminate dissemination of materials, the essential character of which is to degrade sex, will have an eroding effect on moral standards'. Such an inference has been drawn by the legislature in this country, and the 'deprave and corrupt' phrase has been retained for want of any better.[28]

In the case of ordinary obscenity legislation the primary concern of the law seems clearly to be the prevention of moral harm, although the prevention of 'offence' is also a consideration. However, as we saw earlier, it is not easy to arrive at a value-free concept of offence. Lord Devlin concludes that 'neither in principle nor in practice can a line be drawn between legislation controlling the individual's physical welfare and legislation controlling his moral welfare'.[29] He goes on to argue that 'A public morality is a necessity for paternalism, otherwise it would be impossible to arrive at a common judgement about what would be for a man's moral good. If, then, somebody compels a man to act for his own moral good, society is enforcing the moral law.'[30]

Now it might be objected that Lord Devlin's criticisms of Professor Hart's thesis, penetrating though they are, are somewhat out of phase with his own previous position. For it is not, on the face of it, at all obvious that the principle of 'moral paternalism' which he here seems to be advocating is identical with the thesis which he set out to maintain, viz. that 'society may use the law to preserve morality in the same way as it uses it to safeguard anything else that is essential to existence'. To justify morals legislation on the ground that it is essential to the preservation of society seems to be quite different from justifying it on the ground that it protects individuals from moral harm. However, as we have seen, there are a number of possible interpretations of Lord Devlin's thesis and one of the most plausible is that the law has a right to protect the institutions that are judged essential to a given society and the morality associated with them, notwithstanding that such institutions are not necessary to any society whatever. Among

[28] op. cit., p. 260.   [29] p. 135.   [30] p. 136.

the institutions in our society to which the law gives protection is the monogamous family and it is here that there is room for a degree of moral paternalism.

We have been offered two accounts of the purpose of law. According to one it is the protection of individuals from harm, whether inflicted by others or by themselves. According to the other it is the protection of society. To what extent can these two accounts be reconciled? There is, to begin with, the truism that society consists of individuals and that individuals cannot exist independently of society. Moreover, society consists of individuals related to one another in a plurality of interlocking institutions,[31] so that their role in these institutions largely determines their interests and aspirations. The protection of society, then—to start from that end—involves the protection of institutions, at least of such institutions as are important and generally approved. The law's concern for the family is shown by imposing the penalties of the criminal law upon bigamy, by legal recognition of the status of marriage, by legal regulation of divorce and by various legal impediments to 'immorality' where what counts as 'immorality' is determined by the sexual ethic traditionally associated with monogamous marriage. No doubt there is room for controversy as to what this code should be, i.e. as to what form of monogamous marriage we should recognize and what its moral demands are. People may dispute about whether we should recognize the traditional Christian concept of marriage or some other, and to what extent the associated morality should be enforced. But the protection of individuals from harm is not a purpose which can be realized independently of the protection of the institutions under which they live. Most of the sorts of harm from which an Englishman

---

[31] It may be useful to append a sociologist's definition of an institution. Dorothy Emmet paraphrases Talcott Parsons as follows: 'Institutionalized conduct means action involving a number of people with different roles, related to some human interest which is sufficiently recurrent and important for it to be hedged about with legal, and probably also ritual, prescriptions, so as to ensure as far as may be stability in the fulfilment of expectations as to how people will behave and to encourage the finding of satisfaction in ways which are normally approved by other actors in the social situation. Marriage and property would be institutions in this sense.' *Function, Purpose and Powers*, p. 30.

might want to be protected could not be suffered by a Poly-
nesian islander. In being invited to choose between the protection of society and the protection of individuals from harm,
we are, as so often in philosophy, being offered false alternatives.

5

Paternalism and the Enforcement
of Morals

THE time has come to broaden the scope of our inquiry. We took our start from Lord Devlin's lecture on *The Enforcement of Morals* and then went on to consider the response of his critics, notably Professor Hart.

Professor Hart seeks to maintain it as a *principle* that the law should not attempt to enforce morality; though he is prepared to go further than Mill and extend the purpose of law so as to cover the protection of individuals from self-inflicted harm as well as from harm inflicted by others. He is, that is, prepared to countenance a degree of paternalism. Nevertheless, he is quite clear that there is for him a line beyond which the law may not trespass and the enforcement of morals is on the wrong side of that line. Lord Devlin counters by calling in question the possibility of drawing any such line. For if 'paternalism' is restricted to what he calls 'physical paternalism' it is patently insufficient; but, if it is extended to cover 'moral paternalism', the enforcement of morality is in effect conceded.

It looks as if there are two ways in which Professor Hart might meet this attack. He might refuse to make the shift from physical to moral paternalism. As I suggested in the last chapter he might follow Dr. Alex Comfort and supplement physical with psychological paternalism. Or he might make this shift, but deny that 'moral paternalism' entailed the enforcement of morality. We considered last time two difficulties in the way of the first alternative; it is not easy to discover criteria of 'psychological harm' which are value-free; and some of our laws against the exploitation of vice and the corruption of minors are hard to interpret in the way proposed. Yet we may not be willing to jettison these laws.

The second possibility we have still to consider. It raises a question which it may well be thought ought to have been brought to the forefront much earlier. What *is* the enforcement of morality? If, as would appear to be the case, it is preventing people from behaving in certain ways on no other ground than that they are (or are generally thought to be) morally wrong, is it not to be distinguished from moral paternalism, if this means preventing people from having their characters corrupted or degraded? No doubt the two policies would often, in practice, prohibit the same acts, but the grounds of prohibition would be conceptually distinct. Professor Hart argues that

a very great difference is apparent between inducing persons through fear of punishment to abstain from actions which are harmful to others, and inducing them to abstain from actions which deviate from accepted morality but harm no-one. The value attached to the first is easy to understand; for the protection of human beings from murder or violence or other forms of injury remains a good whatever the motives are by which others are induced to abstain from these crimes. But where there is no harm to be prevented and no potential victim to be protected, as is often the case where conventional sexual morality is disregarded, it is difficult to understand the assertion that conformity, even if motivated merely by fear of the law's punishment, is a value worth pursuing, notwithstanding the misery and sacrifice of freedom which it involves.[1]

If we take this passage and emend it to allow for moral paternalism the contrast between this and 'the enforcement of morals' still remains: '... the protection of human beings from murder, violence or other forms of injury, *including moral corruption*, remains a good, whatever the motives are by which others are induced to refrain from these crimes. But where

---

[1] p. 57. The last sentence should have ended at 'is a value worth pursuing'; for Professor Hart's opponents are free to agree with him that in most, perhaps in all, cases the value of enforced conformity is outweighed by the misery and sacrifice of freedom involved. The question at issue between them is whether it is a value *at all*, having any independent weight.

F

there is no harm to be prevented ... it is difficult to understand the assertion that conformity ... is a value worth pursuing.'

Lord Devlin does not take the view that the enforcement of morality is an end in itself. He believes that it is justified only in so far as it is necessary to maintain the 'integrity of society'. What he means by this is not entirely clear, but we have suggested that part of his meaning, at least, is that society has a right to protect the institutions that are judged essential to it and the morality associated with these institutions. That enforced conformity has no value in itself is conceded by both parties to this debate. Indeed, if men are persuaded by threat of punishment to do what is morally right, there is a sense in which what has been enforced is not morality at all. For morality, strictly speaking, involves acting from a moral motive. Considered in this light morality not only ought not to be enforced, it *cannot* be. And this is a point of great importance in connexion with all morals legislation. The attempt to 'make men good by act of parliament' is, strictly, self-frustrating and may tend to ossify morality and weaken the autonomy and creativity upon which genuine morality depends. But it does not follow from the fact that enforced conformity to a moral code has no moral value in itself (and is, in a strict sense, not 'morality' at all) that there is no point in exacting conformity. It may still have instrumental value in two different ways. As Aristotle remarks, 'We become just by performing just acts, brave by performing brave acts.' We are not just or brave until we do the appropriate acts as the just or brave man would do them, i.e. from the developed moral motive, but there is, he believes, a necessary intermediate stage, when we perform the actions without having yet acquired the motive. And at this stage enforced conformity may be necessary. No doubt an enlightened educator will try other devices first, but he cannot bind himself to dispense with coercion altogether. There is also to be considered the moral standard of groups as well as of individuals, and here too it may not be possible to rely solely on the individual's sense of responsibility. The threat of being struck off the register may deter a small minority of doctors from unethical conduct and in this way make it less likely that others will falter. It is somewhat naïve to suppose that an individual's devotion to moral principle is entirely independent of the influence and example of other people, of the 'moral atmosphere' in which he lives. We are generally influenced by what is expected of us. No doubt the man of Kantian moral rectitude will do his duty no matter what his moral environment is like, but, as Kant clearly recognized, such men are rare. Indeed he notoriously exaggerated their rareness.[2] So there may sometimes be a case for enforcing conduct in accordance with morality, not because such enforced conformity is good in itself, or has in itself moral value, but either because it is a necessary stage in the individual's moral development or because it contributes to the moral stability of a society. We do not normally expect society to concern itself directly with the moral development of adult individuals (though the rehabilitation of criminals must involve an element of this), so that the former consideration is of relatively little importance, but it is not clear that we can or should be indifferent to the ethos of our society or that we should rule out in principle, as Professor Hart appears to do, any use of the law to preserve or alter it. There are, of course, grave risks in such a policy, and, in any actual case, these have to be weighed against the arguments for it. However, as Professor Ginsberg points out in connexion with the desegregation laws in the U.S.A., 'It may well turn out that the desegregation laws, if persistently enforced, may help to bring about a change in attitude, in behaviour, *and eventually in moral convictions*'[3] (my italics).

It is not easy at this stage to disentangle the strands of the argument. Lord Devlin clearly holds that the law may, in certain circumstances, be used with a view to preserving, and perhaps also changing, moral attitudes, including those con-

[2] cf. the beginning of the second section of the *Grundlegung*: '. . . If we attend to the experience of men's conduct, we meet frequent and, as we ourselves allow, just complaints that one cannot find a single certain example of the disposition to act from pure duty. Although many things are done in conformity with what duty prescribes, it is nevertheless always doubtful whether they are done strictly *from duty*, so as to have moral worth.' Tr. Abbott, p. 27.
[3] *On Justice in Society*, p. 235.

cerned with sexual morality. Professor Hart appears to reject
this view. He certainly rejects it with respect to sexual morality,
but this may be because he regards sexual morality as 'determined by variable tastes and conventions' or because he regards
it as 'private' in one or more of the senses we distinguished
earlier, i.e. because contraventions of it do no harm or because
it is properly a matter of personal judgement. Since there are
these special reasons why Professor Hart may not wish to
enforce sexual morality, we cannot infer his opposition to the
claim that the law may be used to protect or encourage a
morality which does not suffer from these various limitations,
i.e. a rational, utilitarian morality.

It might indeed seem that those whose 'critical morality' is a
rational utilitarian one must be committed to disregarding
questions of morality altogether in framing legislation, except
in so far as the sheer weight of public opinion compels them
to act (and in this case it is the strength of the feeling, not its
rationality, that matters). The principle involved in such a
case is well stated by Bentham.[4]

But when I say that *antipathies and sympathies are no reason*,
I mean those of the legislator; for the antipathies and sympathies
of the people may be reasons, and very powerful ones. However
odd or pernicious a religion, a law, a custom may be, it is of no
consequence, so long as the people are attached to it.... The
legislator ought to yield to the violence of a current which carries
away everything that obstructs it.

With this solitary exception the sort of actions which, from
their point of view, are suitable for prohibition by law, i.e.
those which harm others or the agent himself, are the same sort
of actions as, by the same criterion, are held to be morally
wrong. Law and morality are two forms of social control aimed
at preventing certain injurious consequences. In some cases the
one kind of control, in some the other will be the more appropriate and each is necessary to the other. The law, as Professor
Hart makes clear, could not function without morality; and
morality would not be possible outside of organized society

4 Quoted by Hughes, p. 663. Bentham, *The Theory of Legislation* (ed. Ogden),
p. 76.

which owes its stability to a public system of law backed by sanctions. For this reason some have suggested that Professor Hart's thesis is simply vacuous. For if morality is concerned only with conduct capable of harming others and the law is competent to proscribe behaviour which harms others, any example which was put forward as illustrating the enforcement of morals could also be described as a straightforward case of preventing harm. Hence the question of enforcing morals can never arise. A utilitarian has the choice of proceeding by way of penal sanctions or of relying upon moral sanctions, but there could be no occasion for enforcing morality.

But this argument is, perhaps, too simple. Is it not conceivable that the law might sometimes be used, and used rightly, to protect a utilitarian morality—to reinforce morality, rather than enforce it? This is, indeed, a possibility which Professor Hart admits.

It may, of course, be argued that, though for these reasons legally enforced conformity is of no value in itself, it is yet indispensable as a means of teaching or maintaining a morality which is for the most part practised voluntarily. 'The fact that men are hanged for murder is one great reason why murder is considered so dreadful a crime.' There is nothing self-contradictory in such theories that the threat of legal punishment is required to create or maintain the voluntary practice of morality. But these are theories requiring the support of empirical facts, and there is very little evidence to support the idea that morality is best taught by fear of legal punishment. Much morality is certainly taught and sustained without it, and where morality is taught with it there is the standing danger that fear of punishment may remain the sole motive for conformity.[5]

Here Professor Hart clearly overstates the case he is attacking. No one wishes to maintain that morality is *best* taught by fear of legal punishment. The most that might be suggested is that morality may, on occasion, need to be supported by legal enactments and even then there is the risk to which he calls attention, 'that fear of punishment may remain the sole motive for conformity'.

[5] p. 58.

This is a complex question, and what is wanted, as Professor Hart says, is empirical evidence. On the face of it, it looks as if a balance has to be struck. Legal penalties may weaken the moral motive in some cases, while reinforcing it in others. Take a case of conduct which is morally objectionable on the plainest utilitarian grounds and is also a punishable offence—dangerous driving. Most people see that it is wrong to drive dangerously, as well as imprudent. Their moral motives need no reinforcing. Others see no wrong in it and will drive dangerously whenever they feel they can get away with it. They are, to some extent, deterred by the threat of penalties. Their moral motive is in no way undermined, because they have none. There are others whose motives are mixed. The moral motive is, perhaps, strong enough to restrain them except when especially tempted, but then it fails. The fear of punishment, however, is a strong enough motive to prevail on these occasions. Does it tend to weaken the moral motive? Perhaps it does, but the risk is worth taking. But then there may be some who are conscientious enough to refrain from dangerous driving so long as others behave themselves, but whose moral motive is not strong enough to withstand the sight of others driving dangerously and getting away with it. This may be for two different reasons. They may be like Mr. Toad, unable to resist a flamboyantly bad example. Or they may be Hobbesian men who recognize an obligation to conform to a code, so long as they have a reasonable guarantee that others will conform and will, if necessary, be compelled to conform.

There may evidently be discernible in some people a sort of motive which is neither a moral motive in the full, autonomous, Kantian sense, nor a mere desire to avoid punishment—a disposition to conform to a pattern of behaviour which is generally accepted, and assumed, rather than thought, to be a good one. Such an attitude is comparable to 'morale' in a team or an army, to the sort of courage that Aristotle attributed to soldiers. It may not be the highest form of morality, but it accounts for a good deal of civic virtue. A lowly, but characteristic, form of it is the English habit of forming queues. I have never forgotten an occasion shortly after the war when I was required to board the Rome–Paris express at Turin. We had chosen Turin because we were informed that three fresh coaches would be added to the train at that point. We could, therefore, go early, get into one of these coaches and secure seats without any trouble. But we had reckoned without the Italian railway authorities. Although the three coaches were clearly visible in a siding when we arrived on the platform, they were not moved until five minutes before the express was due, by which time about twice as many people had gathered on the platform as could possibly secure seats. The subsequent struggle has provided a useful philosophical example ever since. It approximated closely to Hobbes' description of the State of Nature as 'a war of every man against every man'. What astonished me in particular was not the behaviour of the Italians, which to my insular eyes was only what was to be expected, but my own behaviour. I kicked, shoved, and elbowed, thrusting women and children from my path in a manner wholly out of keeping with the character of an English gentleman; and I secured two corner seats.

Reflecting afterwards on my conduct I realized for the first time how much of my normal good behaviour depended upon the conventions and the implicit sanctions of English life. To put it briefly: in England people queue. The queue is, in fact, a simple but by no means primitive institution. There is a tacit agreement among Englishmen that when waiting for anything people form themselves into a line and take their turn according to their position in the line. This principle defines the institution of 'the queue'. The institution has its associated morality; it is wrong to jump the queue. It is wrong even if the individual can get away with it. The institution can survive *some* parasites—habitual queue-jumpers who profit from the fact that others stay in their place. But if enough people jump the queue it will collapse into a free-for-all, which frustrates the purpose of the institution.

In this country queuing has become a settled disposition. People don't generally queue because they feel morally ob-

liged to do so, though they would see the moral point if they
reflected upon it, and feel morally indignant at people who
jump the queue. They have got into the habit. If they were
seriously tempted by examples of flagrant queue-jumping or
lost confidence in the intention of other people to stay in the
queue they would lose the habit. This is where an element of
compulsion might help. The presence of a policeman ready
and able to deter potential queue-jumpers would reinforce the
disposition of the ordinary man—the man waiting for the
Clapham omnibus—to keep his position in the queue.

It is one of the problems of traffic discipline in this country
that there is no such settled disposition on the part of drivers
to avoid troublesome behaviour on the roads, such as exceeding
speed limits and driving after taking drink. The conflicting
arguments about the role of law enforcement in this connexion
have a bearing upon Professor Hart's contention. The Pedes-
trians' Association calls for legal penalties or, where appropriate, for stricter penalties. The Motoring Organizations
favour campaigns to 'educate the motorist'. They fear that to
invoke penal sanctions will be to weaken the motorist's moral
motive and encourage him to think of the police as enemies
and not as allies. The ideal situation no doubt would be a
society of Kantian motorists who refrained from excessive
speed or consumption of alcohol from a sense of duty, based
upon a clear recognition of the social ill effects of such behaviour. To such motorists, wherever they exist, it will make
no difference whether this conduct is punishable by law or
not. They do not need to be deterred by threats of punishment,
and they will not be tempted to inconsiderate behaviour by
the example of others. Nor are they in any need of educating.
There are presumably others who are quite uneducable; they
will be deterred by threats of punishment or not at all. If
society consisted of these two classes alone there would be no
reason why legal restrictions should not be imposed and every
reason why they should. The problem is set by the majority
who fall into neither category. What effect will the imposition
of legal penalties have upon them? In their case will the fear

of punishment become the sole motive for conformity as Professor Hart is inclined to predict? Or will the imposition of penalties strengthen the disposition to avoid such conduct by attaching to it a public stigma, thus reinforcing the 'moral motive' where it is present and adding the sanction of shame to that of conscience? Will potential waverers be more inclined to stick to considerate behaviour if they are not continually confronted with the example of successful infringement and if they have a reasonable guarantee that other offenders will be checked?

As Professor Hart says, what we need is empirical evidence, and speculation on my part is no substitute for it. But enough has been said, I hope, to suggest (a) that what constitutes a 'moral motive' is a question of some difficulty, (b) that it is by no means obvious that in some relevant senses of that expression, the moral motive cannot be assisted by legal action. In the light of this discussion I believe Professor Hart to be over-simplifying in what he says about the value of 'the spirit or attitude of mind which characterises the practice of a social morality'. 'Hence if by the preservation of morality is meant the preservation of the moral attitude to conduct and its formal values, it is certainly true that it is a value.'[6] It is indeed, but society depends for its stability upon a host of customary attitudes and patterns of conduct which have some title to be called 'moral' but which are much more specific and less formal than Hart's 'moral attitude'. In the case of conduct on the roads, I have suggested, the law may have the effect of reinforcing moral attitudes which are straightforwardly utilitarian, and may be, to some extent, *designed* to have this effect. Someone might object that, though this effect of reinforcing morality may be welcome, it ought not to be regarded as within the purpose of the law. Nevertheless, if it counts as an argument *against* a particular law that it tends to weaken moral restraints, it is hard to resist the conclusion that a tendency to strengthen them should count as an argument *for* it, both arguments resting on purely utilitarian premises.

[6] pp. 71–72.

Professor Hart seems to overlook the possibility of this sort of argument. He states the utilitarian principle[7] as it applies to the law on abortion,

> In circumstances such as these it seems most desirable to many critics of the law that the issue should be calmly viewed as one to be decided by consideration of the balance of harm done by the practice, and the harm done by the existing law.... But in fact in England the defence of the *status quo* is rarely conducted on such morally neutral terms: the argument that abortion is itself immoral or will lead to sexual immorality is usually well to the fore in the case against reform.

Yet the extent of sexual immorality is clearly not irrelevant to the number of unwanted pregnancies. A morality of sexual restraint tends to reduce unwanted pregnancies and if a relaxation in the law would tend to weaken such a morality then this is an argument of a purely utilitarian kind against relaxing the law. Precisely similar considerations arise over the question whether contraceptives should be made available freely to teenagers. On the one hand it is argued that since the evil to be prevented is unwanted pregnancies the rational policy is to make available the means of preventing conception. On the other it is contended that such action would seriously weaken an important safeguard against unwanted pregnancies, viz. the existence of a public morality condemning promiscuity. In the case of abortion there is a good deal of evidence that liberalizing the law does not necessarily reduce the demand for illegal abortions and may even increase it, precisely because it weakens the moral restraints upon abortion.

This seems to be one of the points that Lord Devlin is making in his remarks about abortion at the end of his Maccabaean Lecture[8] which some have found perplexing. He says

> If the whole dead weight of sin were ever to be allowed to fall upon the law, it could not take the strain. If at any point there is a lack of clear and convincing moral teaching, the administration of the law suffers. Let me take as an illustration of this the law on abortion. I believe that a great many people nowadays do not understand why abortion is wrong. If it is right to prevent con-

---

[7] *The Morality of the Criminal Law*, p. 47.   [8] pp. 23–24.

ception, at what point does it become sinful to prevent birth and why? I doubt if anyone who has not had a theological training would give a satisfactory answer to that question. Many people regard abortion as the next step when by accident birth-control has failed.

He then goes on to describe the role of the professional abortionist, to whom recourse is made because of the legal difficulties. He points out that the professional abortionist generally receives a severe sentence, because his activities endanger life. He quotes Lord Chief Justice Goddard: 'It is because the unskilful attentions of ignorant people in cases of this kind often result in death that attempts to produce abortion are regarded by the law as very serious offences' and he comments: 'This gives the law a twist which disassociates it from morality and, I think, to some extent from sound sense. The act is being punished because it is dangerous, and it is dangerous largely because it is illegal and therefore performed only by the unskilled.'

Lord Devlin's point here seems to be that nonsense is made of the law if people do not see why abortion is wrong. Let us suppose that abortion is wrong because it attacks the life of the foetus, which will in course of time become a human being. The law extends to the foetus some of the protection it affords to the child when born. It does not regard the foetus as of no more significance than a growth in the mother's body. This is a broadly utilitarian position and does not, so far as I can see, depend upon any peculiarly theological premises, though it derives support from the Christian tradition. If, then, the purpose of the law is to protect the unborn child, this may be done in two ways; by teaching people that abortion is immoral (I do not mean, of course, in all circumstances, but that there is a heavy onus of proof on those who would undertake it); and by legal regulation of the practice. Lord Devlin's point is that the operation of the law will become ineffective and distorted if it is not supported by public morality. But the complementary point can also be made that to relax the law very considerably would weaken the moral restraints even further with the result that the number of illegal abortions would continue to rise, because many more people would regard abortion as simply the long stop for contraception, and demand abortion as a remedy for inconveniences which even the more liberal law did not regard as justifying the operation.

The argument that the enforcement of morals is only legitimate where the morality to be enforced is a rational, utilitarian one, but that such a morality can never need enforcing is, therefore, not wholly convincing. For even a morality which is plainly utilitarian like the morality which condemns dangerous driving or (as I should think) abortion may sometimes need to be reinforced in the manner I have described. Also, as we have seen, the morality which condemns cruelty and unwarranted violence may be the reason for regarding certain kinds of activities as corrupting or degrading; and their corrupting or degrading character may be among the reasons for prohibiting them by law. My examples were cruelty to animals, all-in wrestling and 'the theatre of cruelty'.

Nevertheless it might still be maintained that only a rational, utilitarian morality *should* be enforced or reinforced. And this principle, it might be held, would still exclude a great deal of current 'morals legislation'. In particular it would exclude all reference to sexual morality and to morality of any kind which was influenced by religious considerations. The case for this has been vigorously argued by Professor Louis Henkin,[9] in relation to obscenity. He is, of course, discussing the question in the context of the American Constitution, but his conclusions are capable of being generalized. He considers (and finally accepts) three hypotheses:

(1) Suppression of obscenity is a deprivation of liberty or property ... which requires due process of law. *Due process of law demands that legislation have a proper public purpose; only an apparent, rational, utilitarian social purpose satisfies due process* (my italics). A state may not legislate merely to preserve some traditional or prevailing view of private morality.

(2) Due process requires, as well, that means be reasonably related to proper public ends. Legislation cannot be based on

[9] In the *Columbia Law Review*, 1963, vol. LXIII (1), p. 391.

unfounded hypotheses and assumptions about character and its corruption.

(3) Morals legislation is a relic in the law of our religious heritage; the Constitution forbids such establishment of religion.[10]

Our present concern is with the first: *'Due process of law demands that legislation have a proper public purpose; only an apparent, rational, utilitarian social purpose satisfies due process.'* Like Professor Hart, Professor Henkin is prepared to accept paternalism, 'One may even accept the right of the state to impose restrictions on the individual for his own good— by preventing his suicide, or forcing medical aid, or compelling education; in the context of society these are "rational" ends, reasonably achieved. But how can morals, a non-utilitarian, non-rational purpose, be "reasonable"?'[11] From this it appears that Professor Henkin is willing to allow moral paternalism, so long as the morality involved is rational and utilitarian.

It is only by confining government to what is reasonable that the Constitution and the courts can protect the individual against the unreasonable. Private 'morals', and their 'corruption', ... have profound significance in the life of a nation and of its citizens. But they are not in the realm of reason and cannot be judged by standards of reasonableness; they ought not, perhaps, to be in the domain of government.[12]

Professor Henkin seems to want to distinguish 'private' from 'public' morality by the criterion of rationality,[13] and this calls to mind Professor Hart's distinction between the morality of 'universal values' and sexual morality, based on 'variable tastes and conventions'. The former may be enforced by law, the latter not. 'The morality reflected in most of our common laws has lost its religious origins and shares with the law of the mass of organized mankind a modern, utilitarian social basis.... The constitutional issue begins to stir ... when religious origins are more apparent and persistent, when the law is not common to all civilized nations, when it has no clear utilitarian basis ... polygamy and incest, adultery and forni-

[10] p. 402.   [11] p. 405.   [12] p. 407.
[13] See note on different senses of 'private morality', p. 9.

cation, gambling, intoxication, usury.'[14] He concedes that 'many moral crimes rooted in the Bible—incest, polygamy, usury, perhaps also adultery—may find some secular rationalization or justification ... some concern defined in terms of categorical imperative, of avoiding injury to others, of achieving some social aim.'[15] However, others cannot be credibly rationalized—homosexuality, sodomy, contraception, profanity, sacrilege, immorality, obscenity.

Thus religious morality, as the basis of legislation, comes under a double ban. The Constitution forbids the establishment of religion; and religious morality is, as such, non-rational.

... Perhaps the objection that some morals legislation imposes a religious morality is a facet of the earlier argument that morals legislation cannot be rationally supported. For in substantial part the effect, if not the purpose, of constitutional provisions forbidding religious establishment and guaranteeing the exercise of religion is also to bar the interference of government in the realm of the non-rational, the sacred precincts of personal belief, the personal 'answer', even personal idiosyncrasy. The domain of government, it is suggested, is that in which social problems are resolved by rational social processes, in which men can reason together, can examine problems and propose solutions capable of objective proof or persuasion, subject to objective scrutiny by courts and electors.[16]

The difference between this position and that of Professor Hart seems to be that Professor Henkin is prepared to countenance the enforcement of morals in so far as the morality to be enforced is of the public, i.e. rational, utilitarian kind, whereas Professor Hart rejects the enforcement of morals altogether. Professor Henkin's position is one which Professor Hart, oddly enough, scarcely takes account of. He mentions it only to dismiss it as irrelevant to the dispute which really interests him.

It is sometimes said that the question is not whether it is morally justifiable to enforce morality as such, but only *which* morality

[14] p. 408.   [15] pp. 409–10.   [16] p. 411.

may be enforced. Is it only a utilitarian morality condemning activities which are harmful to others? Or is it a morality which also condemns certain activities whether they are harmful or not? This way of regarding the question misrepresents the character of, at any rate, modern controversy. A utilitarian who insists that the law should only punish activities which are harmful adopts this as a critical principle, and, in so doing, he is quite unconcerned with the question whether a utilitarian morality is or is not already accepted as the positive morality of the society to which he applies his critical principles.... No doubt in older controversies the opposed positions were different: the question may have been whether the state could punish only activities causing secular harm or also acts of disobedience to what were believed to be divine commands or prescriptions of Natural Law. But what is crucial to the dispute in its modern form is the significance to be attached to the historical fact that certain conduct, no matter what, is prohibited by a positive morality. The utilitarian denies that this has any significance sufficient to justify its enforcement; his opponent asserts that it has. These are divergent critical principles which do not differ merely over the content of the morality to be enforced, but over a more fundamental and, surely, more interesting issue.[17]

True enough, as far as it goes. But it is important to notice that in the general debate about 'the enforcement of morals' the positions taken up by Lord Devlin and Professor Hart do not exhaust the field.[18] Lord Devlin says that morality may, subject to certain conditions, be enforced; and he means by morality the positive *de facto* morality of the society in question. Professor Hart says that morality may not be enforced—certainly positive morality may not and he seems not to want to enforce morality, however understood. The moral position which he himself adopts—his 'critical morality'—is of a rational, utilitarian type. It is easy to see that one might agree with Lord Devlin in holding that the enforcement of morals is sometimes permissible, without agreeing with him that the morality to be enforced should be the positive morality of the society. One might hold instead, as Professor Henkin seems to do, that it should be a rational utilitarian morality. One

[17] *Law, Liberty and Morality*, pp. 22–24.
[18] In saying this I am not suggesting that Lord Devlin and Professor Hart suppose they do.

would then be sharing Professor Hart's unwillingness to sanction the enforcement of positive morality, while rejecting his refusal to enforce any morality at all.

This is the position I now wish to consider and it brings me at last within range of my over-all subject. My question is this: on the assumption that 'the enforcement of morals' is sometimes justifiable, are there good grounds for maintaining that the law should not concern itself with sexual morality or with any morality having its roots in religion? But before I tackle it I want to stand back for a while and put the whole debate in perspective. Is it a debate between liberals and reactionaries, or are all the participants recognizably liberals?

6

Varieties of Liberalism

PROFESSOR HART describes himself as a liberal reformer. Lord Devlin is generally agreed to have been a judge of liberal sympathies. Professor Wollheim holds that Lord Devlin's thesis that it is in the nature of society to possess a community of ideas is incompatible with liberalism. As we suggested earlier, it looks as if there are varieties of liberalism.

The classical case for liberalism is that of Milton's *Areopagitica* and Mill's *Essay on Liberty*. It is based on the conviction that it is a necessary condition of the discovery of truth both practical and theoretical that men should be free to test theories by argument and to try different 'experiments of living'. The assumption is that the truth about these matters, although not known, is knowable. Mill went so far as to argue that to prohibit the expression of an opinion contrary to one's own is an assumption of infallibility. In this he was clearly mistaken, as Lord Devlin observes:

... To admit that we are not infallible is not to admit that we are always wrong. What we believe to be evil may indeed be evil and we cannot for ever condemn ourselves to inactivity against evil because of the chance that we may by mistake destroy good. For better or for worse the law-maker must act according to his lights and he cannot therefore accept Mill's ideal as practicable even if as an ideal he thought it to be desirable.[1]

It is one of Mill's most notable characteristics as a philosopher that he prefers logical to material absurdity. He would rather strain the consistency of his system than evade some argument that a reasonable man might put forward. So we find that Mill anticipates this objection.

The objection likely to be made to this argument would

[1] p. 123.

G

probably take some such form as the following. There is no greater assumption of infallibility in forbidding the propagation of error, than in any other thing which is done by public authority on its own judgement and responsibility. Judgement is given to men that they may use it. Because it may be used erroneously are men to be told that they ought not to use it at all? To prohibit what they think pernicious, is not claiming exemption from error, but fulfilling the duty incumbent upon them, although fallible, of acting on their conscientious convictions.... There is no such thing as absolute certainty, but there is assurance sufficient for the purposes of human life. We may, and must, assume our opinion to be true for the guidance of our own conduct: and it is assuming no more when we forbid bad men to pervert society by the propagation of opinions which we regard as false and pernicious.[2]

This objection, as well stated by Mill himself as by Lord Devlin, would seem to dispose of the argument that any censorship of opinions or interference with experiments of living involves the assumption of infallibility, whatever other arguments there may be against them. The argument itself appears to assume that if the legislators *were* infallible they *would* be justified in suppressing contrary opinions. This position was in fact maintained by Plato in the *Republic*. The Guardians in his ideal state have knowledge, which is by definition infallible, and a censorship is to be imposed upon the dissemination of opinions which, since they run counter to knowledge, are necessarily erroneous: 'It is better for every creature to be under the control of divine wisdom. That wisdom and control should, if possible, come from within: failing that it must be imposed from without, in order that, being subject to the same guidance, we may all be brothers and equals.'[3] Plato shows no sign whatever of recognizing that freedom of thought or action has any intrinsic value. He could not concede to freedom the instrumental value which Mill's argument gives it, because there could be no question for him of any truth remaining to be discovered in his ideal state. Nevertheless Mill himself does not draw the conclusion that infallibility would justify suppression. 'We can never be sure that the opinion we are

[2] pp. 80–81, Everyman Edition.   [3] *Republic*, 590.

endeavouring to stifle is a false opinion; and *if we were sure*, stifling it would be an evil still'[4] (my italics). This is because he believes that even if the received opinion is the truth and the whole truth it is likely to be held as an unreasoned prejudice unless it is able to be contested, and the profession of it will lose 'its vital effect on the character and conduct'.

Mill's argument that only in a free society is there a possibility of making new discoveries in the realm of morals as elsewhere and of keeping old truths effectively alive remains a powerful one. It shows that there is a strong presumption in favour of non-interference, though it does not show that that presumption cannot on occasion be rebutted or that a clear criterion can be provided by which we can tell which these occasions are. But the type of liberalism which it represents has been largely superseded by another based on different premises. This is the sort of liberalism which Professor Wollheim stands for. He declares, as against Lord Devlin, that 'the identity, and continuity, of a society resides not in the common possession of a single morality, but in *the mutual toleration of different moralities*'[5] (my italics). What differentiates this type of liberalism from Mill's is the conception of morality which appears in the use of the plural form 'different moralities'. Whereas Mill envisaged a continuous process of experimentation and debate which would, as time went on, refine and develop morality to the common advantage, the new liberalism assumes the possibility of alternative moralities, between which the individual (or group) may choose. The individual's morality is private and personal, not in the sense that it affects no one else, but in the sense that he alone gives it what authority it has. The case for toleration of different moralities, on this view, cannot rest on the hope of discovering by experiment and debate the right answers to moral questions—for the concepts of truth and falsehood are here out of place—some other basis must be found. The case for it is stated eloquently by Mr. P. F. Strawson.[6]

[4] p. 79.
[5] *Encounter*, November 1959, p. 38.
[6] 'Social Morality and Individual Ideal' in *Philosophy*, 1961, p. 1.

What will be the attitude of one who experiences sympathy with a variety of conflicting ideals of life? It seems that he will be most at home in a liberal society, in a society in which there are variant moral environments, but in which no ideal endeavours to engross and determine the character of the common morality. He will not argue in favour of such a society that it gives the best chance for the truth about life to prevail, for he will not consistently believe that there is such a thing as the truth about life. Nor will he argue in its favour that it has the best chance of producing a harmonious kingdom of ends, for he will not think of ends as necessarily capable of being harmonized. He will simply welcome the ethical diversity which such a society makes possible, and in proportion as he values that diversity he will note that he is the natural, though perhaps the sympathetic enemy of all those whose single intense vision of the ends of life drives them to try to make the requirements of the ideal co-extensive with those of common social morality.

The basis for the liberal society in Mr. Strawson's version of it is the intrinsic value of ethical diversity, and Professor Wollheim appears to regard the principle of tolerance as the only moral idea which need be shared in a liberal society.

Dean Rostow accuses Wollheim of using 'liberalism' in a private sense 'for even those societies commonly regarded as most liberal have betrayed *some* departures from the rule of moral permissiveness, in regard to their toleration of unpunished violence, their rules of family structure, their acquiescence in private or public property, etc.'[7] If Professor Wollheim had more space in which to develop his position he would no doubt try to take care of this by allowing, as Mr. Strawson does, for a basic common morality which is necessary for the preservation of any society. Mr. Strawson does this by distinguishing between social morality and individual ideal. What matters for him is that people should be free to create and bring into operation their own individual ideals; but they cannot do this independently of society. They must therefore accept in relation to one another whatever obligations are necessary to the existence of a society. This will constitute a basic common morality upon which may be reared the struc-

[7] p. 193.

ture of individual ideals. This common social morality appears to coincide with Professor Hart's 'universal values', whose recognition, he says, is necessary to *any* society. We discover it again, perhaps, in Professor Henkin's 'rational, utilitarian, morality'. 'One may accept the right of the state to impose restrictions on the individual for his own good ... in the context of society these are "rational" ends, reasonably achieved. *But how can morals, a non-utilitarian, non-rational purpose,* be reasonable?'[8] In Strawson's terminology, how can 'ideals' be reasonable?

What we have here, then, is a broad distinction between a social morality which is rational, utilitarian, and necessary to any society, and moral ideals which are non-rational, non-utilitarian, and peculiarly personal. This distinction is a persistent theme in recent moral and political philosophy.[9] One might almost go further and say that the philosophy based on it is the characteristic position of the contemporary English or American intellectual. Professor Hart appears to recognize it when he says, in *The Concept of Law* that 'It is important to remember that morality has its private aspect, shown in the individual's recognition of ideals which he need not either share with others or regard as a source of criticism of others, still less of society as a whole.'[10] It is easy to see how this can serve as a 'critical morality' by reference to which to determine the relationship between law and morals. For it will preclude any legal intervention in matters which belong to 'private morality', in the sense of what are properly matters for private judgement. It will favour, in Mr. Strawson's words, 'a liberal society ... a society in which there are variant moral environments, but in which no ideal endeavours to engross and determine the character of the common morality.'

The seeds of 'the new liberalism' are to be found in Mill himself. In the third chapter of the *Essay* he champions the

---

[8] p. 405.
[9] cf. R. F. Atkinson, *Sexual Morality*, especially pp. 40–41 and 147, where he distinguishes between 'morality' and 'personal preference'; R. M. Hare, *Freedom and Reason*, especially chapter 8, where he distinguishes 'interests' and 'ideals'. These distinctions do not wholly coincide but it would be hard to deny a family resemblance between them.   [10] p. 179.

value of individuality and originality in a way which comes very close to Strawson's conception of 'variant moral environments': '... different persons also require different conditions for their spiritual development; and can no more exist healthily in the same moral, than all the variety of plants can in the same physical, atmosphere and climate.'[11] But even here he is not indifferent to the question of truth. 'It will not be denied by anybody, that originality is a valuable element in human affairs. There is always need of persons not only to discover new truths, and point out when what were once truths are true no longer, but also to commence new practices, and set the example of more enlightened conduct, and better taste and sense in human life.'[12]

We are not yet in Mr. Strawson's realm of the ethical, that region of 'truths that are incompatible with one another'.

We have seen that the authoritarian society which Mill attacks is based on the Platonic conception of the Infallible Legislator. Plato seems to have drawn the inference, which Mill, to his credit, did not draw, that where the truth is known there is no need of freedom. He resembles the newer sort of liberal in associating freedom with the denial that there is a truth about life. The democratic society, as Plato portrays it, is the society in which all men are free to judge for themselves and judge solely by appearances. The democratic man is one for whom all opinions and interests have equal importance. Such a society is free because no members of it are acknowledged to have greater wisdom than the rest. The individual who is at home in such a society is free because there is no principle in him which has a better claim than any other to determine how he ought to live. The passions are on an equality with reason. Plato has divined (and, perhaps, to some extent determined) the course of subsequent thought. Those who have wanted to make out a case for objectivity have often felt constrained to deny toleration ('error has no rights'); those who have wished to vindicate freedom have often felt obliged to deny objectivity.

[11] p. 125.   [12] p. 122.

It is necessary to ask whether the two types of liberalism we have so far examined are the only possible ones. This is, in effect, to ask whether the case for freedom does turn as Mill thought, on the possibility of our being wrong, or, as Strawson and Wollheim appear to think, on the impossibility of our being either right or wrong. Suppose that we believe that questions of morality are objective in the sense that, if two people disagree about them at least one of them must be mistaken; suppose too, that, in a particular case, we are in fact right. Suppose, for instance, that we are concerned with that part of morality which, according to Mr. Strawson's thesis (accepted, I think, by Professor Hart) is capable of being demonstrated to the extent that the recognition of it can be shown to be necessary to the existence of *any* society. What grounds of principle are there for giving people freedom of opinion and of action?

There is, first of all, the utilitarian consideration, which Professor Hart emphasizes, that deprivation of liberty causes pain. People enjoy, as Aristotle noted, unimpeded activity. This creates one initial presumption in favour of liberty. But it is a presumption that can be rebutted. It may be possible so to indoctrinate or condition people that they do not find deprivation of liberty painful, but rather find it painful to be required to exercise choice. (Our preference for liberty might be said to be culture-bound.) The horror of *Brave New World* is that the people enjoy their degradation.

A stronger argument is therefore needed. It is provided by the Kantian requirement that morality involves treating people as ends, never solely as means. If men are to be moral agents they must be free to make their own choices, and the onus is upon those who would deprive them of this freedom. Kant in isolating this requirement is, as so often, drawing on an earlier tradition. Fr. Eric D'Arcy writes,

... The Thomist finds the seat of all right and all created law in the personal destiny of the individual man. St. Thomas' philosophy of human nature, confirmed and enriched by his theology, led him to conclude that each man has a unique, sovereign value and a unique, sovereign destiny or end which cannot be sub-

ordinated to any other purpose on earth. He would have been
delighted, one feels, with Kant's principle, 'Always treat men as
ends, never simply as means'. This is the controlling principle,
the absolute to which all lesser proposals must be referred, and in
whose light they must be judged.[13]

Father D'Arcy in his book bases his defence of freedom of
conscience upon the individual's duty to follow his conscience.
Such a defence might seem not to cover freedom to act wrongly
in cases where the agent is aware that he is acting wrongly or,
at least, does not believe that he is doing right. This is a point
which Lord Devlin makes against Mill.

Evidently what Mill visualizes is a number of people doing
things he himself would disapprove of, but doing them earnestly
and openly and after thought and discussion in an endeavour to
find the way of life best suited to them as individuals. This seems
to me on the whole an idealistic picture. It has happened to some
extent in the growth of free love. Although for many it is just the
indulgence of the flesh, for some it is a serious decision to break the
constraint of chastity outside marriage. In the area of morals
touched by the law I find it difficult to think of any other example
of high-mindedness.[14]

And later,

Mill believed that diversity in morals and the removal of restraint on what was traditionally held to be immorality would
liberate men to prove what they thought to be good. . . . He con-
ceived of an old morality being replaced by a new and perhaps
better morality; he would not have approved of those who did not
care whether there was any morality at all. But he did not really
grapple with the fact that along the paths that depart from
traditional morals, pimps leading the weak astray far outnumber
spiritual explorers at the head of the strong.[15]

What Lord Devlin here says is valid criticism of Mill's
doctrine that immorality must not be punished by the law for
fear of prohibiting fruitful moral experiments. But in the
course of making this criticism he seems to be denying freedom
any but an instrumental value. Indeed elsewhere he says so
explicitly.

[13] *Conscience and Its Right to Freedom*, p. 198.   [14] p. 107.   [15] p. 108.

Freedom is not a good in itself. We believe it to be good because out of freedom there comes more good than bad. If a free society is better than a disciplined one, it is because—and this certainly was Mill's view—it is better for a man himself that he should be free to seek his own good in his own way and better too for the society to which he belongs, since thereby a way may be found to a greater good for all. But no good can come from a man doing what he acknowledges to be evil. The freedom that is worth having is freedom to do what you think to be good notwithstanding that others think it to be bad. *Freedom to do what you know to be bad is worthless*[16] (my italics).

The question, we must note, is not whether intervention in the activities of those who do wrong knowingly (e.g. commercialized vice, which Lord Devlin is here discussing) is sometimes justifiable; but whether, in deciding *when* it is justifiable, the claims of liberty have any independent weight; if so the claims of liberty to do what? To do what one knows to be right; or to do, also, what one knows to be wrong? It is tempting to say that the one involves the other; that a man cannot be free to do what he believes to be right without *eo ipso* being free to do what he knows to be wrong. But, it may be urged; suppose that we *know* that a man is doing some particular thing which he knows to be wrong, is any justification at all required for stopping him doing it, since, *ex hypothesi*, the choice to do wrong in this instance has already been made? Does the fact that he is acting freely count in the balance at all?

It looks as if, where political liberty is concerned, freedom of conscience is not enough; although it may well be that freedom of conscience has a stronger claim than the mere freedom to do what one wants. Hence in countries where conscientious objection to military service is permitted, steps are taken to discover whether the objection is genuinely conscientious. It will not do for me to appear before a tribunal and say, 'My potential contribution to civilization is such that I cannot conscientiously put myself in jeopardy.' Nevertheless I shall not regard myself as being in a free society if I may, without

[16] p. 108.

reason given, be compelled to do anything to which I do not conscientiously object.

The problem is handled intelligently by Benn and Peters in *Social Principles and the Democratic State*.[17] They quote Mr. J. D. Mabbott:

'I am still doubtful how far liberty is to be valued for itself and how far I am really counting on the ... good effects of variety and experiment to which Mill so often appeals. For if liberty itself is what I value it must have this high merit equally in the bad actions and the good, and I cannot feel sure that, in a case where I knew I was doing wrong, it was at least one good element in the situation that no one tried to stop me.'[18]

On this they comment:

There is something curiously paradoxical about this which derives, in our view, from the language employed. Calling freedom to act 'one good element in the situation', Mabbott treats it as if it were an ingredient in a composite whole, as one might say: 'Though the cocktail was largely made up of vitriol and spirits of salt, the lemon juice was wholesome enough.' But freedom to act is not a constituent of a situation separate from the thing done, and therefore capable of possessing distinct value. What is implied by Mill's principle is not that there is some value in the worst action if it is done freely, but that the onus of justification must always rest on the would-be restrainer, and not upon the person restrained. It is not that freedom of action is necessarily valuable in itself, but that there is always an initial presumption in its favour that must be overcome.

Benn and Peters conclude that:

The maxim 'All restraint, *qua* restraint, is an evil' appears on this analysis, as a way of saying that any restraint of a being who is a fitting subject of moral judgements, must be justified in moral terms.... Consequently, it is a purely formal, or procedural maxim. It indicates where the responsibility for justification lies: it does not help us to decide whether a justification is adequate.[19]

This is eminently sensible and, so far as it goes, true, but does it give the liberal all he wants? Could not Plato himself, indeed, claim to be a liberal on this showing? For his guardians

<hr>

[17] p. 221.   [18] *The State and the Citizen*, p. 62.   [19] p. 222.

would not intervene in the lives of the other citizens unless they were justified in doing so and they could always produce good reasons. What the liberal wants is that some independent weight should be given to individual freedom. To bring out the significance of the metaphor: the liberal wants the initial position to be that the balance is already tilted in favour of freedom, so that whoever would intervene must produce on his side of the balance a heavier weight. It is not enough just to produce *any* weight, however small.

To some extent the considerations Mill notices may help to weigh down the scales in favour of freedom, but they will not do so in the sort of case Lord Devlin has in mind, where everyone knows that what is done is wrong and the reason why it is wrong is so obvious that the moral principle involved needs no constant testing and revitalizing in the public mind. If we feel that the claims of freedom have some weight even in these cases, it must be because we attach positive value to a man's making his own decisions without legal impediment. Thus in the end I am inclined to think that my original impulse was correct. A man cannot be free to do what he believes to be right without being free to do what he knows to be wrong. This does not mean that, as Mabbott seems to suggest, in every bad action there is an element of good, viz. the fact that it is done freely; but simply that a man cannot live the life of a moral and rational being unless he is able to make his own choices, so that restriction of this power by fear of punishment is in itself an evil.

There is, then, as it seems to me, a liberal case which does not rest on the premise that the truth is not known or not knowable. It can, of course, be maintained without any explicit metaphysical background, but it can scarcely pass unnoticed that the intense insistence upon the importance of the individual with which it is associated has not arisen spontaneously outside a Christian culture, and that within the framework of Christian doctrine it fits readily into place. For the terms of the problem as we stated it—how to discover a firm basis for individual freedom when the truth is not merely knowable, but known—are those which determine the theological problem of divine omniscience and human freedom. If the individual has an eternal destiny for which he has been created by God and which God allows him freely to choose, it follows that he has a significance which is not exhausted by any of his natural attributes or by his potential contribution to human knowledge or happiness. If man is made in God's image his freedom and responsibility must be such that they can be subordinated only on terms which pay respect to them. This does not tell us when limitation of freedom is justified, but it does give reason why a clear justification is needed; and it is a reason which does not depend upon indifference to truth.

By contrast the new liberalism appears to base itself primarily upon the absence of any reason for preferring one ideal to another. It is less that there are positive grounds for insisting on freedom, than that there can, in the nature of the case, be no positive grounds for infringing it, except the need to provide the barest substratum of law and order.

There are, then, I suggest, three main varieties of liberalism.

1. A liberalism which bases itself on a conviction about the nature of man and of his destiny and which insists on the need of the individual for freedom to choose the way he shall live. It is a liberalism which has an explicit metaphysical context.

2. A liberalism which is sceptical of religious and metaphysical claims and which sees as the supreme values of human life the discovery of truth and the attainment of happiness. It regards the need for individual freedom partly as a self-evident truth, partly as a precondition of the discovery of truth and the attainment of happiness.

3. A liberalism which is sceptical not only of religious and metaphysical claims but of morality also, except in so far as it is a necessary condition of the survival of *any* society. It sets a high value on human beings and on the ideal projects men desire for themselves, although it does not regard these ideals as, in any sense, objective.

There is thus a consensus as to the value of the human personality and the consequent need to preserve freedom of choice and action, although there are important differences in the ways these values would be defended.

The existence of these varieties of liberalism should be a warning against arguments of the 'only if' type, to which most of us are from time to time addicted. 'Only if the Christian doctrine is accepted that man is created in the image of God and redeemed by Jesus Christ, can the sanctity of the individual be validated.' 'Only if no man or organization is prepared to claim that it has the truth about man and the universe, is mutual toleration logically justified.' 'Only if men cease to regard their ideals as logically incompatible with the ideals of others, can they reasonably refrain from imposing them upon others.'

Of each such argument the possibility of the others would be sufficient refutation. A Roman Catholic who believes that the Church is the repository of final truth; a rational humanist, who holds that in principle, though not yet in practice, men may come to devise a morality that all can accept; a romantic humanist, who must regard such a hope as illusory because he can see no rational way of choosing between ideals; all these may agree in holding political freedom to be of fundamental importance. It is true that their reasons are to some extent different and each will maintain that the others' reasons are, at the worst, false; at the best, approximations to the truth, which his own position fully exemplifies.

It would be very surprising, however, if deep metaphysical differences made no difference at all to the application of the liberal principle. For example, those who believe, with Professor Hart, that sexual morality is largely determined by 'variable tastes and conventions' will not regard it as of any great importance what the sexual habits of a given society are, so long as they do not cause 'tangible harm'. They will not be much exercised by the danger of 'corruption'. Those, however, who believe, as Lord Devlin does, that there is, in these matters, an objective right and wrong and that the sexual morality of a society has a good deal to do with some of its central institutions will take this danger more seriously.

But of even greater relevance to our inquiry is the attitude of the new liberalism to religion. We have already quoted Professor Henkin arguing against the State's support of a religious morality.[20] Religion, says the new liberalism, is a private matter. It belongs to the realm of ideals, not to that of interests. It follows that religious considerations, as they affect morality, should have no place in law making. This is the case we have to examine in the remainder of these lectures.

I want to end the present chapter by raising four queries about the new liberalism. The new liberalism is based upon a fundamental distinction between a social morality which is thought of as a necessary condition of any viable society, and a morality of personal ideals which are for individuals to choose. No ideal should seek to engross the common social morality. The social morality represents, so to speak, an agreed syllabus which everyone is required to take. The personal ideals represent an indefinite array of optional further subjects. The questions I wish to raise are these:

1. Is it in fact possible in logic or in practice to make this distinction? For our ideals normally influence our conception of our interests. Mr. Hare in *Freedom and Reason* gives the following example to illustrate the distinction between interests and ideals:

> Consider the question ... of whether it is wrong for a pretty girl to earn good money by undressing herself at a 'strip club' for the pleasure of an audience of middle-aged business-men. . . . Those who call such exhibitions immoral do not do so because of their effect on other people's interests; for, since everybody gets what he or she wants, nobody's interests are harmed. They are likely, rather, to use such words as 'degrading'. . . . It is a question not of interests but of ideals.[21]

Yet, if I were made guardian of a girl whose parents were going abroad, with instructions to look after her interests, I should not be thought to have discharged my trust if, when

[20] See p. 84.   [21] p. 147.

they returned, I claimed to have served her interests well and added, in explanation, that she was earning a good salary at the local strip club.

2. The second query is one to which, in earlier chapters, we have already given a good deal of attention. Can a society in fact be content with no more than the morality of 'universal values' that is agreed to be necessary to any society whatever? Monogamy, to take the most striking case, is a basic institution of our own society, which, it might be thought, we have every right to protect by law, although it is not necessary to the existence of *any* society and *is* influenced by a religious ideal.

3. The ideal underlying the new liberalism (is this a personal ideal?) is that of promoting the richest possible diversity of individual ideals together with the widest possible range of individual choice and the highest possible degree of personal fulfilment. But are these aims capable of being achieved without social arrangements and organized institutions; and can these be maintained in all cases without legal recognition or protection? Once again the case of marriage is illuminating. In a society which gave its blessing equally to every variety of sexual relationship, marriage as we know it could not survive. As an option it would no longer be available—which is to say that a range of options to be effective must be restricted; and society must choose which it wants to make effective.[22] Perhaps the simile of optional further subjects can serve again as an illustration. If the options are to be effective teaching must be available on an adequate scale for each of them; so the number of them has to be restricted and a choice made on some educational criterion.

4. Is it *quite* clear that the new liberal's theory about the nature of individual ideals does actually imply practical tolerance of other people's ideals? Is it not open to the individual, if he wishes, to take a low view of the importance of individual life and dignity? He will not, of course, be able to claim that

---

[22] cf. The Master of Campion Hall in evidence to the Franks Commission, 'it is destructive for any one university to attempt to combine the excellences of several'. *Report of Commission of Inquiry*, vol. I, para. 245.

any reasonable man should assent to this view, any more than that he should assent to any other personal ideal, but it would seem that he can perfectly well be intolerant of people's ideals, so long as he respects their interests.

Perhaps enough has been said to suggest that the credentials of the new liberalism need careful scrutiny; the more so since its presuppositions lie buried out of sight below many of the positions which are taken up in this debate.

7

What Difference, if any, does Religion Make to Morals?

WE have been considering the question how far, if at all, the law should concern itself with morality and with the somewhat narrower question to what extent, if at all, it should enforce morality. If it is decided that the law should to some extent concern itself with morality and may, sometimes, enforce morality, the further question arises, What morality?

Professor Hart, as we have seen, holds that the law should not enforce morality. He does not, therefore, need to address himself to the question, What morality should it enforce? And he does not consider the wider question, whether the law should concern itself with morality. Lord Devlin believes that the law has a right to enforce morality and that the morality to be enforced is the commonly accepted morality of 'the man in the Clapham omnibus'. It does not matter whence that morality is derived, although Lord Devlin takes it in fact to have been derived from Christianity. As he says of marriage, 'It has got there because it is Christian, but it remains there, because it is built into the house in which we live and could not be removed without bringing it down.'[1] However, Lord Devlin is prepared to envisage a change from the law as it is to the law as it ought to be and this presupposes what Professor Hart calls a 'critical morality' by which what the law ought to be is determined. If this implication is accepted, there arises for Lord Devlin also the question what part religion ought to play in the formation of such a critical morality. He says in his Maccabaean Lecture, 'I suppose that moral standards do not shift; so far as they come from divine revelation they do not, and I am

[1] p. 9.

H

willing to assume that moral judgements made by a society always remain good for that society. But the extent to which society will tolerate—I mean tolerate, not approve—departures from moral standards varies from generation to generation.'[2] From this it looks as if he adopts as his critical morality the Christian ethic based upon divine revelation. Such a morality, as we have already seen, would not, in Professor Hart's view, now seem plausible.[3]

Others, who have taken Professor Hart's side in this debate, have been more ready than he to answer the question, What morality? This is because they are less sanguine than he is as to the possibility of delimiting a sphere of private morality.[4] Thus Mr. Hughes and Professor Henkin maintain that only a rational, utilitarian morality may be enforced, it being clearly implied by Mr. Hughes[5] and explicitly asserted by Professor Henkin[6] that religious morality is, as such, non-rational.

We encounter, then, in this dispute, two theories about the relationship between religion and morality—and by 'relationship' here I mean 'logical relationship'. (We are not concerned with the historical question to what extent our present morality is the product of centuries of Christian teaching, but with the logical question whether all or any of it is logically dependent upon Christian belief.) One theory, which appears to be Lord Devlin's, is that the whole of our morality is logically dependent upon Christian belief. The other, which is that of Professor Henkin, Mr. Hughes and, I suspect, Professor Hart, is that there are two sorts of morality, a morality of 'universal values' whose acceptance is a necessary condition of the viability of any society; and a morality of personal ideals which are essentially a matter of individual choice and are not susceptible of rational discussion. It is not denied that religious belief may affect a man's moral outlook, but it is held that any morality so affected belongs to what Professor Henkin calls 'the realm of the non-rational, the sacred precincts of personal belief, the personal "Answer", even personal idiosyncrasy'.[7]

---

[2] p. 18.   [3] p. 73.   [4] See Hughes, p. 679; Henkin, p. 402.
[5] p. 669.   [6] p. 411.   [7] p. 411.

Since it is held that the law ought to be neutral where the morality of personal ideals is concerned, it follows that no religious morality should influence the law.

These do not, of course, exhaust the possible accounts of the relation between religion and morality. There have been Christian thinkers who maintained that the whole of morality was contained in the Natural Law and that the precepts of the Natural Law were evident to the unaided reason. In their view Christianity provided morality with extra sanctions, but did not affect its content, except in so far as certain obligations are imposed upon members of the Church by divine positive law, such as the requirement of Sunday worship. Hence the State had a right to enforce the Natural Law (although distinct limitations were placed upon its exercise of this right). However, the traditional Natural Law doctrine made certain assumptions which, if not specifically Christian, were certainly theistic, so that it cannot now claim the non-controversial character it once had. Hence Professor Hart speaks quite correctly about '... the more disputable parts of the general teleological outlook in which the end or good for man appears as a specific way of life about which, in fact, men may profoundly disagree'.[8] Moreover the Roman Catholic Church has regarded supernatural revelation as a moral or practical necessity, although not a theoretical one, for knowing the Natural Law without admixture of error;[9] so that neither in theory or in practice does the doctrine of Natural Law, whatever its merits, provide a means of determining moral questions without reference to controversial religious claims.

There exist also forms of secular rationalism very much more hostile to religion than the sort we have been considering, which would base morality solely upon the plainest utilitarian foundations and would leave no room even for personal ideals which were not capable of being justified in terms of 'objective' social criteria. For such a rationalism religion cannot even be tolerated as private fantasy; it must be condemned as public error.

[8] *Concept of Law*, p. 187.   [9] See Stevas, *Life, Death and the Law*, p. 29.

We cannot here attempt an exhaustive treatment of so complex an issue as the relation between religion and morality. The questions we need, at least provisionally, to answer are whether (*a*) morality is wholly dependent upon religion and (*b*) religion has any logical bearing upon morality and, if so, how.

In answer to the first question I propose to be somewhat dogmatic. It seems to me very hard to deny that, in spite of the many cultural differences between human societies, there are certain moral principles and certain moral virtues which have been universally accepted. As Dr. Ewing points out,[10]

Ross's *prima facie* duties have most unfairly been described as just the code of the English gentleman. But it would surely be hard to find a community anywhere in which the fact that you had made a promise, was not regarded as a reason for keeping it, the fact that you had harmed somebody as a reason for making reparation, the fact that someone had intentionally benefited you as a reason for showing gratitude. Even such a perverted system of ethics as that of the Nazis did not reject the *prima facie* duties as such, but gave (bad) reasons for breaking them in a great number of cases.

It is equally hard to deny that their universal acceptance has to do with their social utility. Professor Macbeath provides documentation for this view in his fascinating study of the anthropological evidence, *Experiments in Living*.[11]

Any tolerable form of social life requires that there should be rules governing the relations between persons in regard to such matters as intercommunication, return for services rendered, sex relations, respect for life and property, etc., and that they should be generally obeyed. And the rules contained in lists of *prima facie* obligations are in a general way such obvious conditions of individual and social well-being that most of them are included in the moral codes of most peoples. Their value, and indeed their fundamental importance ... is not in question.

Professor Hart himself has elaborated this conception in a most illuminating way in his discussion of 'the minimum content of Natural Law' in *The Concept of Law*.[12]

[10] *Second Thoughts in Moral Philosophy*, p. 127.   [11] p. 369.   [12] pp. 189 ff.

In face of this evidence it is most unplausible to suggest that this basic platitudinous morality depends for its validity upon religious belief of any kind. Indeed we may go further and say that this morality provides a basis for the criticism and assessment of religious claims. The critic of Christianity who bases his attack upon the moral record of the Church can scarcely be met by the contention that his charge is irrelevant; or that he can, in the nature of the case, find no independent ground to stand upon.

However, the platitudes do not constitute the entire morality of any society, or of any individual. And there are variations possible in the way the platitudes are interpreted and the relative importance that is assigned to them. Moreover, when we take notice of the immense influence that religious belief and practice has exercised in every human society, we shall certainly expect to find that morality has been affected too. Nor is this a purely contingent state of affairs. Any religion claims to give an account of the nature of man and his place in the universe and makes moral demands which derive from this account. Every religion, as Professor H. A. Hodges has put it, contains a metaphysic, an anthropology, and an ethic. It is interesting to observe that Professor Hart recognizes this fact in a passage we have already had occasion to notice.[13]

No doubt a critical morality based on the theory that all social morality had the status of divine commands ... would not for obvious reasons now seem plausible.... Nonetheless the attempt to defend the legal enforcement of morality on these lines would be something more than the simple unargued assertion that it was justified. It is worth observing that great social theorists like Burke and Hegel, who were among those most anxious to defend the value of the positive morality and customs of particular societies against utilitarian and rationalist critics, never regarded the simple assertion that these things were of value as adequate. Instead they deployed *theories* of human nature and history in support of their position.

The relation between Christian doctrine and Christian ethics is a good deal more complex than is suggested by the

<hr>
[13] *Law, Liberty and Morality*, p. 73.

formula 'all social morality has the status of divine commands', but it is true that Christian moralists from St. Paul to Reinhold Niebuhr have been concerned to work out the ethical implications of their theology. Since the subject matter of this reflection is man in society it is to be expected that the platitudes will find their place in any scheme of Christian ethics, for they are the 'humanly necessary' conditions of any tolerable society. But, as I have said, not all morality is platitudinous and even that which is may be variously understood and interpreted according to different estimates of human nature and the human condition. A religious interpretation of human life may illuminate the morality of the platitudes to the extent that it deepens understanding of the human nature upon which the platitudes are founded. But it may also be expected to go beyond the platitudes by providing insights into human nature, which are not available to the 'natural man' and so giving rise to moral insights which are not available to him either.

In a society which has been deeply influenced by Christianity one would expect to find a good deal of moral agreement between believers and unbelievers, both because the platitudes are common to all reasonable men and because the language and institutions of such a society incapsulate many distinctively Christian attitudes. There are, it has often been remarked, noticeable differences between a Catholic and a Protestant atheist: even more so between a Christian and a Mohammedan atheist.

There are disagreements not only between Christians of different traditions, but also between Christians and secular humanists and between secular humanists themselves; and more often than not people are unable to explain in terms of any clearly articulated 'philosophy' why they adopt the moral position they do. In fact most individuals are not wholly consistent in their morality, which they have derived from diverse and sometimes incompatible sources. Certainly those critics of Lord Devlin are right who accuse him of exaggerating the homogeneity of modern British society.

It is not in dispute among Christians that love is the supreme Christian virtue and that it is founded upon the conviction that every person is a child of God, made in his image, redeemed by Jesus Christ and destined for eternal life. We have seen how this conception has influenced the liberal idea. Nevertheless it has never been a simple matter how to apply it. Does love free us from all rules; or are rules needed for the working out of the principle of love in the complexities of human society? Is the law of love all that we need or does it require to be supplemented with other independent moral principles? Love demands that we consider each man's good, but can it tell us in what his good consists? [14]

In point of fact the commonest criticism of the Christian Churches made by humanists, with the support of some liberal Christians, is that, in the name of love, they incline to moral attitudes that are harsh and inhumane. They oppose euthanasia, preferring to leave men to die slowly and in agony. They either oppose abortion altogether or wish to keep it under strict control. They are prepared to condemn the partners of an unhappy marriage to lifelong misery rather than grant them divorce on request. This, at any rate, is how it looks to the critic.

In each of these cases there is, upon closer examination, a substantial utilitarian case for the more conservative position. Thus, although there may be individual instances, in which the right thing to do is to bring a painful terminal illness to an end, the dangers of abuse, were such a principle given recognition, are so great as to justify the gravest doubts as to the wisdom of it. [15] The moral condemnation of abortion rests chiefly on the recognition that the foetus, though not yet a human individual, is in process of becoming one and cannot be treated as simply a growth in the mother's body. And in this case, too, as the experience of Japan indicates, free access to abortion may induce an attitude of mind which regards a new

[14] See Paul Ramsey, *Deeds and Rules in Christian Ethics*.
[15] See *Decisions About Life and Death: A Problem in Modern Medicine*, pp. 22–23.

pregnancy as a threat to the well-being of the mother and her family, simply because it happens to be inconvenient.[16]

The conviction that abortion is always or as a rule morally wrong has, historically, been associated with Christian reverence for life, but it does not require any specifically Christian or theistic premise. One does not have to be a Christian in order to believe that a human being in the making is to be treated differently from any other organic growth. Similarly with euthanasia, one does not have to be a Christian to maintain the sanctity of human life. Yet there are distinctively Christian, or at least, theistic considerations which have a bearing on these matters. The traditional Christian belief is that:

the disposal of human life is in God's hands, so that man has not absolute control over it: he may have the use of it and he may, therefore, prolong it, but he may not destroy it at will ... Nor can this be required by love, for if a man is not free to take his own life when, so far as he can see, it serves no further use, he cannot be required by love of his neighbour to do for him what he could not rightly do for himself.[17]

The same sort of reasoning makes it difficult for the Christian to countenance abortion on the sole ground that a defective child is likely to be born.

What lends colour to the secular humanist's accusation of severity in these problems about life and death is the Christian's unwillingness to give overriding importance to the prevention or relief of pain. Where for many secular humanists the claims of compassion point unambiguously to the cessation of a painful situation the Christian sees life also as a task to be performed where some good can be achieved, even if it be only that of dutiful obedience. Both attitudes have their characteristic corruptions. The Christian view can decline into an inflexible moralism; the humanist into a superficial sentimentalism. But each represents a value which is worthy of respect. Even if theistic assumptions are left on one

[16] See *Abortion: An Ethical Inquiry.*
[17] *Decisions about Life and Death*, p. 28.
   These pamphlets are published by the Church Information Office for the Church Assembly Board for Social Responsibility.

side it is far from easy to determine which of these attitudes makes for greater happiness in the long run. It may, at first sight, seem obvious that men will be happier in a society whose institutions and ideals attach primary importance to the prevention and relief of suffering and the attainment of happiness. But it may be the case that people who are accustomed to regard pain and death simply as evils to be avoided and controlled will find life less satisfying than those who take it for granted that such obstacles will be encountered and should be borne with fortitude. Life will continue to be difficult, no matter what we do, and it may be a poor preparation for dealing with what cannot be avoided to regard it as the worst of evils.

Questions of life and death are among the two main sets of controversial issues where Christian ethics bears upon matters taken into account by the law. The other set is those concerned with sexual morality. Here too it is possible to hold what is in substance a Christian position without basing it upon specifically Christian, or even theistic, beliefs. Such is what Mr. R. F. Atkinson calls 'the Western norm',[18] i.e. 'that conception of marriage and sexual relations generally which is at least the point of departure for discussions of sexual morality in the more or less "advanced" Christian or post-Christian societies of Europe and the New World. The content of the Western Norm or ideal is familiar enough. It is that sexual relationships shall be exclusively heterosexual, and that no sexual activity shall take place outside monogamous unions which are, intentionally at least, life-long.'

Mr. Atkinson observes that '... the Western norm has not only been widely disregarded so far as sexual *behaviour* is concerned but ... it has also not infrequently, explicitly or implicitly, in one respect or another, been challenged *in principle*'. In the twentieth century and, to some extent, in the nineteenth this is, of course, true. But, as a counterpart to this judgement, it is worth quoting Peter Laslett's impression of the situation in pre-industrial England. 'The impres-

[18] *Sexual Morality*, p. 45.

sion left by the beginning of research into the sexual conduct of the men and women of pre-industrial England is as follows. They obeyed the code. They did so whether they were Protestants or Catholics, Anglicans or Separatists, townsmen or countrymen, commoners or gentry.'[19] 'Nothing approaching promiscuity can be inferred from the evidence in either England or France at any time or for any age group, and the whole issue seems peculiarly inappropriate to the study of life in the traditional world.'[20]

Although this consensus no longer obtains, present disagreements do not run along a line neatly drawn between Christians and secular humanists. Some liberal Christians favour 'the new morality' and many humanists support the traditional ethic. The traditional restriction of sexual intercourse to marriage can be variously defended. There is, first of all, the need for children to be born and reared in a secure and loving home, in which the whole-hearted commitment of each parent to the other and to the children is not in doubt. As an argument against pre-marital intercourse this depends to a large extent upon the absence of a completely reliable contraceptive. But even if this were available, there is no guarantee that it would be used. Still, it might be argued that the dangers would not then be great enough to justify restriction upon liberty. But the traditional view rests also upon the belief that a necessary (though not, alas, a sufficient) condition of the profoundest love between the sexes is the mutual trust that goes with a life-long commitment. In such a relationship the sexual act itself serves not only for the procreation of children, but also for the expression and reinforcement of their love. Thus it appears to those who take part in it to have a quasi-sacramental character.

To the Christian it has, in fact, a sacramental character as the appropriate expression of a life-long union. And it is here that specifically religious concepts make their entry. Marriage is thought of as 'ordained for the procreation of children and the mutual comfort and consolation the one ought

[19] *The World We Have Lost*, p. 131.   [20] p. 130.

to have of the other', and the sexual organs are thought of as *designed* for this purpose. Hence use of them outside marriage is to be condemned. There are many who, without benefit of theology, accept this estimate of the function of sex and feel that sexual intercourse without a deep personal relationship is, in some way, sub-human. They are reluctant to regard this simply as a personal preference, so that sexual activity has only as much significance as the partners choose to give it. To this extent the ideal which they accept is in debt to the Christian conception. To express this ideal, as one is tempted to do, in terms of 'the purpose of marriage' or 'the function of sex' is to presuppose a teleological theory of ethics of a sort which consorts best with an explicitly theistic metaphysic. As Atkinson rightly observes 'in so far as functional assertions enjoy religious support, the problem of justification is transferred to the credentials of the religious or theological system in question. This is one of the several points at which religion impinges on morality.'[21] The Christian 'theology of marriage' is concerned primarily with the life-long commitment of one man and one woman to each other. There are practical reasons of obvious weight why normally this commitment should be a public act, by which the parties are seen to undertake their mutual responsibilities. But from the moral point of view what matters is the commitment itself. It is this which constitutes the marriage, and in the marriage service it is the couple who together make the sacrament; the priest witnesses it and blesses the union. Thus pre-marital (i.e. pre-ceremonial) intercourse between engaged couples might, if they had, in fact, vowed life-long union, be from a moral point of view, in no essential way distinct from marriage.[22]

The 'Western norm' has been attacked as unrealistic, but, for a social rule, it has the signal advantage of clarity. For a person to answer honestly the question 'Am I in love?' or 'Have I a deep personal relationship?' is remarkably difficult. It is not much easier to determine whether sexual relations in a given case are likely to harm anyone. In both instances the

[21] p. 66.   [22] cf. Paul Ramsey, *Deeds and Rules in Christian Ethics*, p. 33.

temptation to self-deception is strong. The marriage vows make quite explicit what is intended and call not for introspection but for commitment.

Thus the Christian attitude to sex has a good deal more coherence than is suggested by Professor Hart's expression 'variable tastes and conventions'. Indeed in the present confused situation there is no single alternative which commands anything like the same degree of support.

I have argued that theological arguments do have a bearing upon moral questions and I have tried to show what this is with respect to some of the issues that the law is concerned with. In each case I have drawn attention to the relationship between theological and utilitarian arguments, and have assumed that this relationship is a source of strength. It has, however, sometimes been maintained that it is a source of weakness. Thus Professor Alasdair MacIntyre observed in connexion with divorce,

> When theologians are considering the problems of divorce, for example, their argument nowadays has to be two-pronged. Divorce, they will suggest, is objectionable both because it increases human unhappiness and because it violates the divinely ordained harmony of marriage. I am not in the least concerned here with the rights and wrongs of divorce. What I want to bring out is how fatal the use of this type of argument must be to theology; fatal because one prong of the argument transforms the theologian into a social scientist and the other preserves his theology at the cost of making it humanly irrelevant for most people.[23]

Why is this type of two-pronged argument fatal? The point presumably is that only the appeal to the 'divinely ordained harmony of marriage' is a genuinely theological argument, and, if it suffices, then no considerations drawn from social science can touch it. If, however, appeal is made to social factors, then the whole issue becomes one for social science, and theological considerations are irrelevant. If the theologian preserves his independent role by leaving social factors out of account, he succeeds only in making his theology socially sterile; but, as

[23] 'A Society without a Metaphysics', *Listener*, 13 September 1956, quoted by D. L. Munby, *The Idea of a Secular Society*, p. 26.

soon as he tries to remedy this by looking at the facts of the case, he enters a realm in which conclusions can only be reached on non-theological grounds.

This argument deserves to be taken very seriously, since, explicitly or implicitly, it is widely influential. People tend to dislike religion, when it 'interferes' with the practical business of life; they dislike it often whether they are religious or not. 'Let theologians stick to their theology,' they think, 'and not meddle in matters which are not their concern.' Hence religious thinkers who make a serious attempt to bring the Christian tradition into fruitful relationship with the genuine social problems of the time are often resented more than those who stand aloof. *Critics* of religion, in particular, often regard it as something approaching intellectual sharp practice to adapt traditional teaching to the needs of the time. And they have, indeed, some reason to be suspicious, since such adaptations sometimes involve re-interpretations so drastic as to be no longer recognizable as Christian doctrine. But it is difficult not to feel that, apart from this quite reasonable suspicion, the critic likes theology to be doctrinaire enough to be discounted with impunity. We are more comfortable with stereotypes. We are happy to know that our theologians are doctrinaire and irrelevant, just as we are happy to know that our dons are remote and ineffectual.

There are, then, widespread prejudices with which this argument conspires; but what we have to consider is the argument. What assumptions does it make? Two at least, one about theology, one about social science. About theology it assumes that it represents a system of ideas accepted on authority about whose interpretation there is no doubt and which can be applied to the world, so to speak, *neat* and without any examination of the natural features of the world to which it is to be applied. About social science it assumes that it represents, at least in principle, a closed system, capable of yielding definite answers to practical social problems without reference to moral and metaphysical beliefs. If theological thinking took the form of a simple appeal to authority and if social science were a complete and wholly self-contained system, then indeed the theologian could only venture into the social sphere at the cost of abandoning his theology. But is either of these assumptions true or even plausible?

To begin with social science. The social sciences, as they are practised today, do not presuppose a metaphysical determinism and do not give much support to it. Their methods are generally statistical and they would not claim, and do not even try, to cover the entire range of human activity and experience. But even if they were to do so there is no indication that they would be able to dispense with explanations in terms of human purposes and ideals and thus become wholly 'scientific' as that word is understood in the natural sciences. It is true that there are some who believe this may be possible, but theirs is as yet a metaphysical belief rather than a scientific theory. Moreover, when social science is harnessed to practical social problems, the problems are those of a particular society and inevitably reflect, in their formulation, the institutions and ideals of that society. We have already noticed Lady Wootton's scepticism about the possibility of a value-free concept of mental health. It is interesting to notice her equally frank avowal of this further fact. In the introduction to *Social Science and Social Pathology* she writes:

No one can embark on a discussion of anti-social behaviour without making assumptions as to the criterion by which any specific actions are defined as such; and these assumptions are bound to reflect, not only the norms of a particular culture, but in some degree also, the subjective preferences of the person who makes them; and even where standards are much the same, actual manifestations will vary.[24]

She continues:

In some respects at least, the norms of this contemporary British culture are clear enough. Plainly ours is a society which believes (or believes that it believes) in hard work, sobriety, ambition, cleanliness, order and social advancement; which sets a high value upon property and upon the conquest of the material environment; and which, if not strictly monogamous, at least professes a deep concern

[24] p. 13.

for the integrity of the biological family. These are, moreover, values which we share with much of the Western industrial world, and which seem to be increasingly admired in many 'under-developed' but 'developing' areas both in the East and in Africa; and they are values which are reflected on both sides of the iron curtain. A definition of social pathology, therefore, which sees this as failure to conform to these standards has at least the merit of being widely understood.[25]

It looks, then, as if the assumption about social science in MacIntyre's argument does not hold. What of the assumption about theology? Christian theology involves the belief that God who has created the world and who has created men in his own image for relationship with him, has revealed himself uniquely in the life and death of Jesus and continues to do so through the Church which is the Body of Christ under the guidance of the Holy Spirit. However much theologians may differ as to the extent to which God may be known through the created order without special revelation, it is implicit in the Christian claim that the purposes of God are to be realized in and through the created order and that men are granted some insight into these purposes. If this is so, it would indeed be very strange if such a revelation had nothing to say about the created order itself or if empirical investigation of the created order were wholly irrelevant to our understanding of the divine purpose.

The point can perhaps be made by means of a simple parable. Supposing a stranger comes into a Kingdom with whose laws and institutions he is unfamiliar. He asks an inhabitant, 'Why do you do things in this way?' The inhabitant replies, 'Because this is the way the King commands; moreover, our institutions have the following practical advantages', which he then proceeds to enumerate. The stranger objects. 'Your argument,' he says, 'is two-pronged; you justify your institutions by reference to the King's authority and also by considerations derived from social science. This procedure is fatal to the King's authority: for it either makes the King a social scientist or it deprives his authority of any relevance to your affairs.' It

[25] p. 14.

is not difficult to see how the inhabitant will answer this. 'We have reason to believe,' he will say, 'that our King is very wise and that is why we accept his authority. Our independent investigations in social science lend support to this belief of ours, in so far as we are able to rely upon them, although we do not make the mistake of supposing that our social scientists are omnicompetent. We have need, of course, to interpret the King's commands, so as to apply them intelligently to the changing problems of our society and we find it a useful rule to interpret them in such a way that they make sense. In doing this we receive valuable help from the King himself.'

There is no need to stress the limitations of the parable, but it does, I think, fairly make the essential point, which is that the insights of theology are not to be regarded as prescriptions to be applied unreflectively to a world with which they have no affinity. If Christianity is true it should illuminate precisely those human needs which men are found in experience to have, and this not by accident but because the God of revelation is also the God of nature.

There is, I suspect, a further reason why some are tempted to repudiate this conclusion. It is this. If factual investigation can be appealed to in support of theological insights—if the proven evils of broken homes can be adduced in support of the 'divinely ordained harmony of marriage'—then, were this support to be lacking or were evidence to the contrary to accumulate, the theological position would to that extent be weakened and might, in principle, even be refuted. There is a marked reluctance on the part of some people to expose religious doctrines to this sort of test. I have tried to deal with this problem elsewhere.[26] Here I can only say dogmatically that I believe the risk must be taken. It is simply the price of involvement with life, and it is a price which, I think, Christianity has agreed to pay in claiming to be a historical religion.

[26] 'The Justification of Religious Belief', in *The Philosophical Quarterly*, 1961.

8

Some Concluding Comments on the Debate

We have encountered in the course of our exploration a number of proposals for delimiting the scope of the law's concern. First there is the attempt to distinguish a realm of private morality which is not the law's business. Since everything of importance that a man does may affect the welfare of others, whether or not it is done in private, this attempt appears not to succeed. Moreover, as Mr. J. R. Lucas[1] has pointed out, the proposed principle would not do the job required of it. It is both too narrow and too wide: too narrow because a man needs freedom in far more than a private sphere, e.g. to practise his religion and to express his political opinions; too wide because sexual emotions are powerful and can have important repercussions outside the private sphere.

The suggestion is next made that the law should concern itself only with non-controversial 'universal values', those values which are common to all societies (or, at any rate, all civilized societies), since no society is viable without them. The proposal is attractive and we have seen reason to believe that there *are* moral platitudes which merit the title 'universal values' and which can be said to be essential to any organized society. Professor Hart's willingness to regard it as a necessary truth that 'a shared morality is essential to any society' is a consequence of his recognition of what he calls 'the minimum content of Natural Law'. However, there are a number of reasons why reliance on non-controversial 'universal values' is not enough. The first is that whereas such principles as the sanctity of life are, abstractly considered, not controversial,

[1] *The Principles of Politics*, p. 342.

their application is often controversial. As we have already seen, abortion and euthanasia are controversial issues among people all of whom accept the protection of human life as among the duties of the State. They differ, however, in the case of abortion, as to whether the foetus shares the right to life, which is unequivocally conceded to the child once it is born; in the case of euthanasia, as to whether life is to be preserved when it appears to offer no prospect but pain and suffering. Differences arise, that is, as to the scope of the principle, and as to the importance to be accorded to it in relation to other values such as relief from pain. In the current controversies about safety on the roads, it is apparent that people differ as to the extent to which they are prepared to subordinate convenience or excitement to the preservation of life. If we thought the preservation of life to be of overriding importance we should ban motor traffic altogether. In such matters the State, since it is agreed to have a concern with the preservation of life, has necessarily to adjudicate, and, in so far as differences about the scope of the platitudes or their priorities are traceable to divergent views of a religious or 'philosophical' kind, these latter cannot be left wholly out of account.

But a more important reason is that, although 'universal values' are necessary for the existence of any society, they are not sufficient for the regulation of any particular society. The preservation of society implies the preservation of certain institutions whose precise form is variable from one society to another and is generally determined by the ideals of the society in question, which have, of course, very often been religious ideals. Chief among these institutions are those of marriage and property. Some form of the institution of marriage is essential to any society—this much is a platitude—but it is evident that there are wide variations possible in the form it takes. Even where a particular form of marriage is securely entrenched as is monogamy in Europe and the United States and, increasingly, elsewhere, there are many controversial issues about it and about the sexual morality associated with it. Yet it would be highly implausible to argue that the law ought not to protect monogamy on the ground that it is possible for a society to be viable without it. Lord Devlin's concern with preserving what he calls 'the essentials of a society' is wholly intelligible if this is taken to mean 'the essential *institutions* of a society'.

If this is conceded, as I think it must be, a further alternative may be proposed. It may be suggested that the values with which the law should concern itself, although not 'universal' in the sense just mentioned, should nevertheless be 'rational'. We have seen this requirement emphasized by Professor Henkin and Mr. Hughes. This insistence on 'rational' values would tend, and is intended, to rule out two possibilities: (i) that the values behind the law should simply be the *de facto* positive morality of the society in question, as Lord Devlin proposes, (ii) that the values behind the law should be in any way influenced by religious belief.

Clearly a great deal depends on how this position is interpreted. Its proponents may be maintaining simply that when a change in the law is under consideration it should be approached in a reasonable spirit. Arguments should be logical, irrelevant appeals should be excluded, all possible empirical evidence should be collected and assessed in an unbiased fashion. Such an approach is indeed incompatible with the mere counting of heads or uncritical acquiescence in existing attitudes, whatever they may be, or unreflecting deference to established authority. It is accordingly opposed to Lord Devlin's thesis (on one interpretation of it) and, I should say, rightly opposed to it. But it excludes religious contributions to the discussion only upon the assumption, itself controversial, that religious claims are necessarily irrational. Rationalism of this modest variety must surely be accepted and is, indeed, essential to the democratic process.

But rationalists often appear to intend more than this. They seem to suggest that the existing institutions of a society are to be held suspect unless they can be shown to be rationally defensible by certain fairly narrow utilitarian criteria. Their programme approximates to what Professor Popper calls 'utopian social engineering' and is, to that extent, open to the criticisms which he directed against that conception. His argument is well summed up by Mr. Atkinson,[2]

Very sweeping 'utopian' proposals for social change are irrational because they are, inevitably, leaps in the dark. Reformatory proposals can only be rationally founded upon, and hence are limited by our capacity to make, social predictions, to say, with reason, what will happen if such and such is done. But all we can make with confidence are rather short-term predictions in narrow fields. Crudely, we have to assume that all else will remain the same when we try to estimate the effects of some particular change.... Generally speaking, the more radical the change proposed, the less likely are other things to remain the same, the harder it is to predict what will happen, and the harder therefore rationally to assess the merits of the proposal.

Atkinson goes on to mention a further point which is even more directly relevant to our inquiry.[3]

A further point with the same tendency is the 'functionalist' thesis that institutions are so intimately and intricately interlinked into complex social wholes, that making any change in one institution will have largely unforeseeable ramifications throughout the whole of society. Family structure is, for instance, closely bound up with the property system, the laws and customs relating to inheritance, to the principles for the division of labour between men and women, etc. and etc. For an example of a possible ramification take the suggestion that the economic emancipation of women tends to reduce the stability of marriage. Such functionalist considerations tend to suggest that even 'piecemeal' innovations may have largely indiscernible effects.

This warning (which neither Atkinson nor Popper takes as an argument for extreme social conservatism) conveys, perhaps even better than Lord Devlin does himself, why existing institutions are not to be lightly interfered with. But there is also a more positive reason, viz. that, as Professor Hart puts it, 'There is a presumption that common and long established institutions are likely to have merits not apparent to the rationalist philosopher.'[4] In other words, not only should we not exaggerate our power to make changes on the basis of

[2] p. 56.   [3] p. 56.   [4] p. 29.

rational decision, we should also not underestimate the possible
rationality of traditional institutions, even where it is not
immediately apparent.

The sort of rationalism we are here considering assumes
that a clear-cut, readily discernible division is possible between
what is rational and what is not.[5] The assumption appears to
be that there will be, or should be, ready agreement as to what
is and what is not 'rational' and that religious belief is, by
common consent, non-rational. But those who hold religious
beliefs will not, for the most part, concede that these beliefs,
together with their moral implications, are non-rational. The
secular humanist, they will be inclined to argue, is free to
maintain that there is, in fact, no rational basis for religious
belief, but he cannot expect this to be accepted as a non-
controversial statement. He can properly require religious
thinkers to obey the canons of rational discourse, but he cannot reasonably expect them to allow all the important questions to be begged against them from the start.

A different, and more sophisticated, version of the secularist
thesis is that which underlies 'the new liberalism'. Religion,
on this showing, belongs to the realm of ideals, which are
essentially expressions of personal preference. It ought not,
therefore, to be allowed to influence the common morality,
which alone should be reflected in the law. This doctrine has
for some an air of self-evidence but, as our argument has suggested, the central distinction between ideals and interests
cannot be used in the way intended, because a man's ideals, or
those of his society, largely determine his conception of his
interests and hence his conception of what constitutes harm.
We are not generally prepared to regard our ideals as beyond
rational criticism or as valid for no one but ourselves. It appears
otherwise through a failure to distinguish between vocational
and moral ideals. Vocational ideals answer the question, 'How

[5] Thus Professor Henkin, as already quoted, 'Only an apparent, rational,
utilitarian social purpose satisfies due process. A state may not legislate
merely to preserve some traditional or prevailing view of private morality.'
(p. 402.) 'One may accept the right of the state to impose restrictions on the
individual for his own good ... But how can morals, a non-utilitarian, non-
rational purpose be "reasonable"?' (p. 405.)

shall *I* live?' and are thought to be in no way binding upon others. Moral ideals answer the question 'How should *a man* live?' A Christian, for example, may recognize a vocation to the priesthood or to celibacy without in any degree regarding a similar choice as incumbent upon everyone. But he does not think of chastity as, in this sense, a matter of individual choice, nor, if he did, would it be for him a moral virtue.

The issue is too complex and difficult to be taken further here. I do not want to beg the question against those who would extend the range of private preference to include more than it traditionally has.[6] I simply wish to point out that it is scarcely possible for anyone who takes religion seriously to acquiesce in its being treated as, in this sense, a purely private matter.

What we discover as we explore the variety of views about the relation between law and morals and between religion and morals is that they reflect moral differences. This is scarcely surprising. But it is also true, I think, that these moral differences are generally associated with differing beliefs about man and 'the human condition'—not always very explicitly associated, because we are not in this country given to explicit statement. These more profound differences affect not only what we take to be the content of morality, but also our conception of its nature and scope, and, indeed, the language we employ in talking about it. Readers of the correspondence columns of *The Times* can scarcely fail to notice the extent to which the very vocabulary used tends to separate the disputants. It would not be an exaggeration to call our choice of vocabulary a moral act. In this situation professional philosophers have not always been as helpful as they might have been. They have too often assumed that philosophy consists in the neutral analysis of concepts and this has led them to suppose that they can illuminate these controversial questions without becoming involved in them. In effect they have become involved without knowing it. For example, the doctrine that religious beliefs are to be interpreted as private preferences, which we have seen to be characteristic of the new liberalism,

---

[6] See Atkinson, pp. 38 ff.

CONCLUDING COMMENTS ON THE DEBATE 125

is associated with the philosophical critique of theological statements which, in varying degrees of sophistication, has been widely influential in this country since the publication in 1936 of Ayer's *Language, Truth and Logic*. This critique has undoubtedly contributed to a clearer understanding of certain features of religious discourse, but to most of those who have a serious concern with religious belief it has seemed gravely inadequate. They may, of course, be doing no more than expressing the alarm we experience when, as J. L. Austin used to put it, 'we feel the firm ground of prejudice slide away beneath our feet'. But it is not possible to judge from a neutral standpoint on which side the prejudice lies. Whether its apparent (or alleged) inability to make sense of religion is a defect in a philosophical theory will be decided differently according to the individual's own assessment of the religious case (including, of course, the philosophical arguments of those who accept it). The debate continues and is conducted by the participants with mutual respect and a common devotion to the cause of truth. But few who are familiar with it would care to say that at this theoretical level there is more agreement than there is at the level of practical decision. There is, perhaps, less. What is conspicuously the case is that people are prepared to listen to one another, to take one another's arguments seriously and sympathetically, in brief to be reasonable.

What distinguishes the political from the academic forum is that decisions have to be taken. Where legislation is in question we must, as Lord Devlin urges, act according to our lights. It is not possible here, any more than in theoretical discussion, to delimit a non-controversial zone. But it is possible to seek reasonable compromises based on mutual respect and with a common concern for truth and for individual freedom.

In the light of this discussion we can see the need to distinguish between the demand for rational procedures and the adoption of 'rationalist' positions. We are committed by the traditions of a free society to accepting the former; we are not committed to the latter. This does not mean that secular humanists cannot, or should not, maintain that their doctrines provide the soundest basis for liberalism; or that they cannot, or should not, seek to eliminate the Christian influences in our legal system and elsewhere. It simply means that they may not claim that the free institutions and democratic procedures to which we are all committed coincide with their own particular conception of a liberal society.

It is beyond dispute that the traditional institutions of our society have been deeply influenced by Christianity, so that any movement to reform them must take account of the Christian ideas underlying them. What is needed is a 'critical attitude' as Professor Popper[7] understands it.

The other possibility is a *critical* attitude, which may result either in acceptance or in rejection, or perhaps in a compromise. Yet we have to know of and to understand a tradition before we can criticise it, before we can say: 'We reject this tradition on rational grounds.' Now I do not think that we could ever free ourselves entirely from the bonds of tradition. The so-called freeing is really only a change from one tradition to another. But we can free ourselves from the *taboos* of a tradition; and we can do that not only by rejecting it, but also by *critically* accepting it.

Whether in a particular case the decision favours critical acceptance or critical rejection or some compromise between the two, a careful investigation of all the relevant considerations is called for, and these will sometimes include theological ones. The way in which such an inquiry might proceed is set out with typical moderation by Professor Ginsberg. He says (speaking about the Wolfenden Committee),

The committee admit that they found great difficulty in discovering what standards people appeal to in forming their opinion about what is offensive or injurious or inimical to the common good. They in their turn do not explain how they hope to arrive at 'a just and equitable law' in the matter with which they are concerned. Their task does not extend, they say, 'to assessing the teaching of theology, sociology, or psychology', and nothing is said of moral philosophy. But this is what has to be done in any serious effort to deal with proposed changes in the law in matters about which moral opinion is divided. A double inquiry is needed; a critique of the moral principles and assumptions and an inquiry

[7] *Conjectures and Refutations*, p. 122.

into the relevant facts and tendencies. We cannot assume that public or positive morality is unchangeable or beyond criticism, or that we know enough of the forms of social adjustment that are possible. If law and morals are to be linked we need to reach agreement on the procedure to be followed in bridging the gap between them. This I take to be the task of a critical jurisprudence, and a study of recent work on controversial issues—as, for example, capital and corporal punishment, birth-control, euthanasia, divorce—will show that such jurisprudence must make increasing use of the social sciences combined with philosophical analysis of the extent and nature of any disagreements there may be on matters of moral principles.[8]

What Professor Ginsberg here advocates may seem to be the plainest common sense, as, indeed, I think it is. But it can by no means be taken for granted. Thus Dr. Glanville Williams writes, 'For the legislator, it seems sufficient to say that theological speculations and controversies should have no place in the formation of rules of law, least of all rules of the criminal law which are imposed upon believers and non-believers alike.'[9] Here he appears to deny that theological considerations should be allowed to enter at all into the public debate that precedes legislation, simply because they *are* theological considerations. It is important to be quite clear what is being asserted. Dr. Glanville Williams *may* just be arguing that religious doctrines are, as a matter of fact, false and should be denied any influence upon the law for that reason. It goes without saying that this is, if accepted, the strongest possible reason. It is entirely open to secular humanists to try to persuade us to reject Christianity and to accept a different world-view. They are free to convert us to a fresh set of values, or rather, since most of us harbour an internal conflict about these matters, to strengthen one set in us at the expense of another. But Dr. Glanville Williams may not be taking his stand upon the falsehood of Christianity. He may be maintaining that theological considerations, *whether based on truth or falsehood*, should play no part in the debate; and this con-

---

[8] *On Justice in Society*, p. 233.
[9] *The Sanctity of Life and the Criminal Law*, p. 208.

I

tention must, I think, be resisted. For this is to suggest that it should be one of the conventions of the debate that in the criticism of our traditional institutions one set of considerations, which have historically been of the greatest importance and are still widely influential, should be on principle excluded. It is hard to see how the process of criticism to which Professor Popper attaches importance can be effectively carried on if any attempt to understand the religious basis of an existing institution and to reconsider it in the face of contemporary social realities is to be ruled out from the start. Dr. Glanville Williams has written elsewhere[10] that 'the degree to which the British can still be described as Christian is a complex question', and indeed it is. Even if, for the sake of argument, it is conceded that ours is a secular society, it is important to be clear what this means. It means, without doubt, a society in which Christianity has no privileged position. In such a society, for example, the Christian conception of marriage cannot be the basis of our marriage law, simply because it is Christian. But Dr. Glanville Williams appears to be insisting that ours is, or should be, a secular society in a very much stronger sense than this, viz. that it should be a society in which non-theological utilitarian principles should occupy a privileged position. Thus he writes, 'libertarians do not necessarily attack the enforcement of utilitarian morality; they attack the enforcement of theological, non-utilitarian morality, which they probably deny to be morality in truth.'[11] Here again it is not *absolutely* clear that Dr. Glanville Williams is expressing the view I have been attributing to him. He may simply be urging, as he has every right to do, that his opponents in the debate are mistaken; not trying to exclude them from the debate. It is only fair to add that in his book *The Sanctity of Life and the Criminal Law* he does not act as if he held this view, but shows scrupulous care in examining the particular religious doctrines with which he disagrees.

[10] 'Authoritarian Morals and Criminal Law', in the *Criminal Law Review*, 1966, p. 142.
[11] p. 144.

It is, I think, quite clear that, whether or not we are in any sense a Christian society, we are not in this stronger sense of the word a secular society. Our legislators may listen to Lady Wootton; they may also listen to the Archbishop of Canterbury, and to the views of Christian laymen as well as to the views of non-Christians. The proposal that we are considering is, put crudely, that they should be permitted to listen to Lady Wootton, but not to the Archbishop of Canterbury (unless, perhaps, he forgets his theology). What grounds could there be for such a rule?

1. That the Archbishop's presuppositions are not rational, whereas Lady Wootton's are. But whether, or to what extent, this is so, is precisely the chief point at issue between them. Is it among the principles of a free society that the issue should be prejudged in her favour?

2. That the Archbishop's values, even if arguably rational, are not purely human values, but the State is concerned only with these. It is necessary here to distinguish between religious and moral duties. The State should not impose religious duties; but the human values with which it is admittedly concerned are open to different interpretations and some of these are influenced by religious belief. A choice may, therefore, on occasion have to be made and the legislator must in the end choose according to his lights (with due consideration for those who disagree).

3. That many do not share the Archbishop's presuppositions. But many also do not share Lady Wootton's. It is desirable that, so far as possible, people should not be subjected to legislation with which they fundamentally disagree, but this cannot be accepted as an overriding principle. A Marxist in a capitalist society may reject the whole basis of its property system, but this provides no decisive argument against giving this system the protection of the law. It may be suggested that religion is so controversial a matter and people's religious beliefs so little, in practice, affected by argument that, whatever the theoretical considerations may be, it is better to leave 'theological speculations and controversies' on one side. This

argument has a good deal of force; but it should not be exaggerated. It is equally true that people are slow to change their political allegiance and are relatively impervious to argument in political discussion also, but we do not seek to keep Socialist and Conservative convictions out of politics, nor do we generally stigmatize these as non-rational. Professor Ginsberg calls for a double inquiry, 'a critique of the moral principles and assumptions and an inquiry into the relevant facts and tendencies'. It would be a curious convention which systematically discouraged the attempt to subject moral principles to reflective scrutiny in the case of some of those which are most widely held and deeply felt.

4. There is a further consideration of some weight. It has to do with Mill's suspicion of 'infallible' legislators. It is felt that religious claims, unless firmly confined to the 'private sphere', are essentially authoritarian in tendency. Mild and reasonable as the Archbishop now is he comes of theocratic ancestors; he is in principle committed to the belief that in essential matters the truth is known, and this belief is an enemy to liberty. I have argued earlier that it is a mistake to suppose that liberalism depends upon scepticism or agnosticism. There is a Christian case for the free society. Moreover both Christians and secular humanists would do well to bear in mind Mill's insistence upon the invigorating power of continuous criticism. It is very difficult for a contemporary Christian to deny that some developments which the Church now welcomes were pioneered against ecclesiastical opposition; or for rationalists to assess the debt they continue to owe to the widespread influence in our society of Christian conceptions. Christians cannot set limits to the operation of the Holy Spirit; rationalists would be very rash to underestimate the degree of reason involved in traditional institutions.

If 'democracy presupposes a readiness to consult all experience, to respect all persons as sources of claims and arguments,'[12] it would seem that it cannot refuse on principle to

[12] S. I. Benn and R. S. Peters, *Social Principles and the Democratic State*, p. 353.

listen to any who have a serious case to state and who accept the conventions of a free society. In arguing this I have been concerned to meet the case of those who insist on the admissibility only of what they call 'rational, utilitarian' arguments. This has led me to some extent to over-emphasize, as they do, the part played by explicit rational argument in reaching democratic decisions. Professor Karl Britton writes about Mill,[13] 'He over-emphasizes the importance of rational argument. Political differences are not merely differences of opinion which can be settled by debate: they commonly involve differences in moral judgement of an ultimate kind: they are conflicts of will and feeling and character. And the purpose of deliberation, in democracies of the British model, is less to reach a "solution" than to show exactly where the lines of division lie, and what sort of compromise will in fact be accepted by all the different parties in a peaceful manner.' This is fair comment. It would be idle to expect to achieve agreement in many of these controversial matters, though this is no reason for not taking informed discussion as far as it will go or for assuming that there cannot, even in principle, be good grounds for preferring one world-view to another. Whether this is so is itself another controversial question. What it does suggest is that a neat distinction between those arguments which are and those which are not rational and utilitarian is not likely in practice to be achieved; and even in theory there are liable to be as many forms of utilitarianism as there are divergent conceptions of what is valuable in human life.

The preceding discussion has inevitably been somewhat abstract. It may perhaps help if I try to illustrate it in terms of the metaphor which Lord Devlin uses when he writes of monogamous marriage that 'it has got there because it is Christian, but it remains there because it is built into the house in which we live and could not be removed without bringing it down'.[14] The social structure of any historical society may be compared to an old and very rambling house which has grown over the centuries in a variety of styles, but which has never-

[13] *John Stuart Mill*, p. 108.   [14] p. 9.

theless a distinct character of its own. It is, shall we say, an English house, and could never be mistaken for anything else. It possesses, presumably, certain fundamental elements of structure without which no house could stand. These correspond to the 'universal values' which must be recognized in any conceivable legal system. But these basic essentials are not enough to enable any particular house to perform its function. This house, then, has certain important features, which are of a general type found in virtually all houses, but whose detailed working out is peculiar to it. They correspond to such institutions as those of marriage and property whose precise form is variable from one society to another, though no society is entirely without them. It has also many other valuable, if less important features, some structural, some purely ornamental, to which those who live in it may be attached—or at least some of them may be. It is, as I have said, a large house and the people who live in it may disagree more or less sharply about the policy they should adopt towards it. They may have conflicting views, for example, as to how much of the structure, as it exists at any time, should be regarded as essential to the architectural scheme and protected accordingly, and how much should be left to individuals to modify according to their taste. Some look upon a house as a machine to live in and claim the widest possible liberty in refashioning their own corner of it to suit their private style of life. Others regard as of great importance the whole character and atmosphere of the place, which they feel to be dependent on all sorts of details, which to the rest are superficial and more or less dispensable. They are, shall we say, libertarians and traditionalists. There are differences, too, about the extent and rapidity of change. Some are anxious to convert the house as rapidly as possible to what they think the present age requires, even if it means taking some risks with the structure. Others, impressed by the antiquity of the building, and the difficulty of discovering where one piece of it ends and another begins, are extremely chary of any precipitate alteration. It is not that they expect the whole building to collapse if any part of it is touched, but simply that they do not know what delicate equilibrium might be upset if people once started tampering with it. These are radicals and conservatives. Add to this the fact that agreement is hard to achieve as to the changes that *ought* to be introduced, and further divisions become apparent. Some want to alter the building in order to bring it up to date, but in such a way as to perpetuate its characteristic merits in a contemporary style. Others are largely out of sympathy with the traditions which it represents and want to eliminate all traces of it as soon as practicable. How should these various parties settle their disagreements?

One party will be inclined to draw a strict line between what affects the structure as a whole and what should be a matter for individual choice and to construe 'what affects the structure as a whole' as narrowly as possible, by identifying it with whatever is essential to any house whatever. The difficulty with this is that there are features essential to *this* house which do not satisfy the proposed criterion and it is by no means easy to secure agreement as to the extent of their ramifications. Another party, conceding that such a line cannot easily be drawn, proposes that 'rational utilitarian' alterations only shall be entertained, thus hoping to rule out of the discussion all arguments based on what others believe to be the traditional architectural virtues of the building. They are equally hostile to such arguments whether they favour the straightforward reproduction of an earlier style or its re-interpretation in a contemporary idiom.

Three points are worth noting. The first is that some of the differences of opinion may be pretty fundamental. They may be differences about the whole purpose of a house—is it no more than a convenient background for people's private lives or is the relationship between the house and those who live in it one of close reciprocal interaction? The second is that, in spite of these fundamental differences, on particular issues the lines of controversy may cut across them. The people living in the house do not neatly divide into distinct and altogether homogeneous parties. The third is that many, perhaps most of them, are clearer about where they stand on these particular issues than they are about the more fundamental questions, to which they may never have explicitly directed their attention.

It stands to reason, I think, that these people will be well advised to make the fullest use of the technical advice given them by architects, engineers, and surveyors as to the likely effects upon the building as a whole of any changes they think of making, though they will also be wise not to regard these experts as infallible. But when they have done this they must make up their minds to act and, given the multiplicity of their points of view, the final decision is likely to be, and ought to be, a more or less untidy compromise.

To return finally to the question of 'the Enforcement of Morals' which was our starting point. Our discussions suggest the following conclusions:

1. The function of the law is not only to protect individuals from harm, but to protect the essential institutions of a society. These functions overlap, since the sorts of harm an individual may suffer are to some extent determined by the institutions he lives under.

2. The law should not punish behaviour on the sole ground that it is, or is generally thought to be, immoral; but it cannot be, in all respects, morally neutral. Not only does it presuppose certain 'universal values' whose scope and relative importance it has sometimes to determine, but its commitment to 'paternalism' requires it to adopt some conception of what tends seriously to corrupt the ethos of society, whether in the form of cruelty, unwarranted violence, race hatred, or 'commercialized vice'.

3. The morality which the law presupposes is not beyond criticism and ought to be open to informed discussion and debate together with the fullest use of social research where this is relevant.

4. The protection of institutions, and legitimate concern for the ethos of society, may sometimes justify what I have

called 'the reinforcement of morality'. This applies as much to a morality that is plainly utilitarian as to any other. But the onus ought to lie heavily upon those who would interfere in private behaviour, even though a clear line cannot be drawn between public and private morality.

The refusal to draw such a line is often taken as the mark of an illiberal attitude. It is necessary, therefore, to indicate what are the considerations which legislators should bear in mind. They include these principles: [15]

(a) So far as possible, privacy should be respected.

(b) It is, as a rule, bad to pass laws which are difficult to enforce and whose enforcement tends, therefore, to be patchy and inequitable.

(c) It is bad to pass laws which do not command the respect of most reasonable people who are subject to them.

(d) One should not pass laws which are likely to fail in their object or produce a great deal of suffering, or other evils such as blackmail.

(e) Legislation should be avoided which involves punishing people for what they very largely cannot help.

These are among the reasons why opinion has moved in favour of reforming the law on homosexual practices between consenting adults. In the area of the law concerned with 'commercialized vice' these considerations are less decisive and the danger to society appreciably greater. Whether the law is effective or not in this area, whether much damage would be done if the law did not intervene, are questions which can to some extent be answered by empirical research. But in the end a moral judgement is required. The mark of a free society is not that it abstains from making such judgements, but that it enables them to be made freely and responsibly after the fullest possible discussion.

I return to the point that I made at an earlier stage about the two protagonists in this debate. They represent different

[15] cf. J. R. Lucas, *The Principles of Politics*, p. 347.

moral standpoints, but they are both, recognizably, liberals. They agree on the importance of freedom. They agree on respect for truth. They agree about the style, courteous and restrained, in which their differences should be discussed, and in their contributions to this debate notably exemplify it.

Select Bibliography

Abortion, An Ethical Discussion, Church Information Office, 1965

Atkinson, Ronald, *Sexual Morality*, Hutchinson, 1965

Benn, S. I. and Peters, R. S., *Social Theory and the Democratic State*, Allen & Unwin, 1959

Comfort, Alex, *Sex in Society*, Duckworth, 1963; Penguin Books, 1964

D'Arcy, Eric, *Conscience and its Right to Freedom*, Sheed & Ward, 1961

Decisions about Life and Death, Church Information Office, 1965

Devlin, Patrick, *The Enforcement of Morals*, Oxford University Press, 1965

Emmet, Dorothy, *Rules, Roles and Relations*, Macmillan, 1966

Ginsberg, Morris, *On Justice in Society*, Penguin Books and Heinemann, 1965

Hart, H. L. A., 'Immorality and Treason', *The Listener*, 30 July 1959, p. 162; reprinted in *The Law as Literature*, edited by L. J. Blom-Cooper, Bodley Head, 1961
—*The Concept of Law*, Clarendon Press, 1961
—*Law, Liberty and Morality*, Oxford University Press, 1963
—*The Morality of the Criminal Law*, Oxford University Press, 1965

Henkin, Louis, 'Morals and the Constitution: the Sin of Obscenity', *Columbia Law Review*, 1963, vol. 63, p. 393

Hughes, Graham, 'Morals and the Criminal Law', *Yale Law Journal*, 1961, vol. 71, p. 662

Lucas, J. R., *The Principles of Politics*, Clarendon Press, 1966

Mill, John Stuart, *On Liberty*, London 1859. Reprinted in *Utilitarianism, Liberty and Representative Government*, J. M. Dent & Sons (Everyman's Library, No. 482), 1910

Popper, K. R., *The Open Society and its Enemies*, Routledge, 1945, 1952, 1957 (later editions revised)
—*Conjectures and Refutations*, Routledge & Kegan Paul, 1963

Rostow, Eugene, 'The Enforcement of Morals,' *Cambridge Law Journal*, November 1960, p. 174; reprinted in *The Sovereign Prerogative*, Yale University Press, 1962

St. John-Stevas, Norman, *Life, Death and the Law*, Eyre & Spottiswoode, 1961

Strawson, P. F., 'Social Morality and Individual Ideal,' *Philosophy*, January 1961, p. 1

Williams, D. G. T., 'Sex and Morals, 1954–63,' *Criminal Law Review*, April 1964, p. 253

Williams, Glanville, *The Sanctity of Life and the Criminal Law*, Faber & Faber, 1958
—'Authoritarian Morals and the Criminal Law', *Criminal Law Review*, March 1966, p. 132

Wollheim, Richard, 'Crime, Sin and Mr. Justice Devlin', *Encounter*, November 1959, p. 34

Wootton, Barbara, *Social Science and Social Pathology*, Allen & Unwin, 1959

Index